UNDERSTANDING RELIGION AND SPIRITUALITY IN CLINICAL PRACTICE

The Society of Analytical Psychology Monograph Series

Hazel Robinson (Series Editor)
Published and distributed by Karnac Books

Other titles in the SAP Monograph Series

Understanding Narcissism in Clinical Practice
in the Psychoanalytic Process
   Hazel Robinson & Victoria Graham Fuller

Understanding Perversion in Clinical Practice:
Structure and Strategy in the Psyche
   Fiona Ross

Understanding the Self–Ego Relationship in Clinical Practice:
Towards Individuation
   Margaret Clark

Understanding Boundaries and Containment in Clinical Practice
   Rebecca Brown & Karen Stobart

Understanding Dreams in Clinical Practice
   Marcus West

Orders
Tel: +44 (0)20 7431 1075; Fax: +44 (0)20 7435 9076
Email: shop@karnacbooks.com

UNDERSTANDING RELIGION AND SPIRITUALITY IN CLINICAL PRACTICE

Margaret Clark

KARNAC

First published in 2012 by
Karnac Books Ltd
118 Finchley Road, London NW3 5HT

British Library Cataloguing in Publication Data

A C.I.P. for this book is available from the British Library

ISBN 978 1 85575 870 4

Edited, designed and produced by The Studio Publishing Services Ltd
www.publishingservicesuk.co.uk
e-mail: studio@publishingservicesuk.co.uk

Printed in Great Britain

www.karnacbooks.com

CONTENTS

Margaret Clark trained as a psychodynamic counsellor and a psycho-analytic psychotherapist at WPF Therapy before she trained as a Jungian analyst at the Society of Analytical Psychology in London. She has been a training therapist for the Foundation for Psychotherapy and Counselling (WPF), a training analyst and supervisor for the British Association of Psychotherapists and a training analyst of the SAP. Her previous book in this series was published in 2006: *Understanding the Self–Ego Relationship in Clinical Practice: Towards Individuation*.

This series of clinical practice monographs is being produced primarily for the benefit of trainees on psychotherapy and psychodynamic counselling courses. They are produced with the hope that they may help students a little with the psychodynamic "Tower of Babel" encountered as they embark on training.

It can be a time-consuming task for students to access all the pertinent books and papers for any one clinical subject. These single-issue monographs have been kept relatively brief and, although not comprehensive, aim to bring together some of the major theorists and their ideas in a comprehensible way, including references to significant and interesting texts.

Much of the literature provided for students of psychotherapy has been generated from four- or five-times weekly analytic work, which can be confusing for students whose courses are structured on the basis of less frequent sessions. The authors of these monographs have aimed to hold this difference in mind by offering clinical examples that are not based on intensive work. A decision was taken to maintain the terms "therapist" and "patient" throughout.

When a training is "eclectic", that is, offering several different psychodynamic perspectives, a particular difficulty can arise with the integration, or, rather, *non*-integration, of psychoanalytic and Jungian analytic ideas. The teaching on such trainings is often presented in blocks: a term devoted to "Freud", another to "Jung", "Klein", and so on. It is frequently the students who are left with the job of trying to see where the ideas do and do not fit together, and this can be a daunting, even depressing, experience.

SAP analysts are in a better position than most to offer some help here, because its members have been working on this kind of integration since the organization was founded in 1946. Although retaining a strong relationship with "Classical" Jungian scholarship, SAP members have evolved equally strong links with psychoanalysis. Those readers who are unfamiliar with Jungian terms may wish to consult the *Critical Dictionary of Jungian Analysis* (Samuels, Shorter, & Plaut, 1986), while those unfamiliar with psychoanalytic terms may turn to *The Language of Psychoanalysis* (Laplanche & Pontalis, 1988).

The authors are Jungian analysts who have trained at the Society of Analytical Psychology, with extensive experience of teaching both theory and practice. We are indebted to our patients. Where a patient's material is recognizable, their permission to publish has been given. In other cases, we have amalgamated and disguised clinical material to preserve anonymity. We have also borrowed gratefully from the work of our supervisees in many settings.

We thank Karnac Books for their continued support and patience in bringing the series to publication. I want to end by thanking my colleagues within the SAP for their work so far, and for their work to come.

Hazel Robinson
Series Editor

Introduction

Out of the myriad definitions of spirituality and religion, this book uses the following: these definitions are expanded later in the Introduction.

It takes a wide definition of *spirituality* to include our longing to find meaning and significance in our daily lives, to grasp a purpose beyond the physical for being alive at all. This longing is "as real as hunger and the fear of death" (Jung, 1928, par. 403). Along with the physical, the emotional, and the intellectual/rational, it is the fourth major mode by which we respond to our environment and to the facts of our existence. Our need for spiritual satisfaction is just as urgent as our need for physical, emotional, and intellectual satisfaction. Spirituality is not necessarily about "uplifting" or "good" experiences; the spiritual can also be demonic, terrifying and destructive. It can include the denial of any purpose or significance in our being alive. Spiritual experience is like emotional experience: it is amoral. Only the use that the whole personality makes of it renders it morally good or bad.

It is necessary to distinguish spirituality from its frequent associations with God and with religion. *Religion* is understood here as a particular formulation of a spiritual quest which includes a focus on "God", and the many different religions, sects, and cults reveal how varied is people's concept of "God", how varied are the answers given to the question, "Who, or What, is God?", and, hence, how varied are the goals of each individual's quest. The use of the capital "G" is intended to reflect the importance most people give to the idea of God. It is usually just as important to a person to say "I do not believe in God" as it is for another to say "I do believe in God". Moreover, to many people, the term God refers to some sort of personal being, and even for those for whom this is not so, there is often a residue from childhood of being presented with a person whose name is God.

It is religion that is more likely to make a therapist's unconscious hackles rise, or, indeed, their conscious ones. The book will explore such difficulties, and will also consider the kind of challenges which spirituality brings to the therapist. Clinicians without an understanding of the importance to our well-being of the satisfaction of our spiritual longings might well be seduced and limited by a patient's own limitations. When the patient expresses their solution to their search for meaning and significance in their lives as finding an exciting and satisfactory sexual partner, or having a baby, or leaving home and getting a job, or making a lot of money, or becoming ill and being looked after, then the clinician could locate such longings in a familiar part of their theory, such as Oedipal triumph, idealization, regression, separation–individuation, sublimation, a denial of reality. But, in doing this, they might not respond to the powerful underlying urge to find a meaning for being alive at all.

Spirituality and religion in counselling and psychotherapy trainings

Most therapists will have received no training in thinking about these matters psychodynamically. The physical, the emotional, and the intellectual aspects of our developmental processes and of our current ways of experiencing life are examined in great detail in all counselling and psychotherapy trainings. We devote years in our trainings to understanding various manifestations of sexuality, for instance, or of our relationship to our mother, and what these may mean in terms of internal object relations, and whether we consider them pathological or not; similarly, we consider our own reactions to such material from a patient, what is a "neurotic" countertransference and what is a countertransference picking up the patient's own feelings.

About cultural differences, there might be something. But about spirituality and religion, there is usually nothing. It is rare for any trainee to be asked to examine, or understand, their own spiritual standpoint. It is even more rare for them to be required to consider that this, whatever it is, is relative and not absolute. There are some honourable exceptions. Gruber notes that the transpersonal model of the Centre for Counselling and Psychotherapy Education is based on the assumption "that our essential nature is spiritual" (Gruber, 2009, p. 31). And at the training institute WPF Therapy, trainees are given a whole year of seminars on Ontology (the study of being), where they consider together their personal spiritual position on matters as diverse as religions, morality, abortion, sexual orientations, marriage, the death penalty, free will and determinism, mortality, time . . . But in most trainings, it is as if the spiritual aspect is considered so remote from important, everyday feelings and behaviour that any examination of them clinically is irrelevant, and a waste of time.

With religion also, the training deficiency goes back for generations. One unfortunate participant at a workshop I gave reported that her supervisor considered her patient's material about religion as neurotic, irrelevant, or delusional, and would not discuss it in supervision. Presumably, the supervisor's own training therapist had not taken his feelings about religion and spirituality any more seriously.

Religion, however, matters. It is integral to cultural identity, and causes untold suffering in "honour" killings and forced marriages in Asian families, in a Jew who wishes to "marry out", a Protestant who does not wish her children to be brought up as Catholic according to the religion of her husband, a celibate Catholic priest or nun, or a young Muslim man or woman torn between their traditional beliefs and practices and the attractions and opportunities of a Western lifestyle.

Spirituality

The spiritual aspect of the psyche is separable from emotion and intellect, even though it cannot be experienced without an admixture of body, emotion, or intellect. In the practice of Yoga, for instance, we see them all combined: Yoga is a spiritual discipline, expressed through the body, controlling the emotions, and focusing the mind. We could think of anorexia, for example, as a dysfunctional spiritual system: an anorectic person tries to solve her emotional problems through physical control, but the wish for control, of self and others, becomes so absolute that this in itself attains spiritual significance and becomes the purpose of being alive; indeed, it might become so great a purpose that it is more important even than being alive.

Spirituality is closely linked to imagination, and manifests frequently in images, as well as in a wide range of emotional experiences from temperate to ecstatic or despairing, and in intellectual formulations, which we call theology or philosophy. Spiritual experiences are a well-testified, apparently universal, human experience, through all cultures, at all historical times of which we have knowledge, shared by children, the middle-aged, and the elderly. They can be induced by drugs, ascetic practices, or deep contemplation. Or they just happen. They can occur through brain damage, epilepsy, or near-death experiences.

Words might be used, such as "divine", "sacred", "numinous", "transcendent", and "holy", to try to "place" spiritual experiences. They encompass experiences of what we perceive as another world, or another dimension to our world: the hearing of voices, the seeing of visions, out-of-body experiences, mystical or ecstatic experiences, seeing ghosts, feeling that prayers are answered, the perception that God is punishing, or saving, a person, being called to a vocation, contact with the dead, ideas of reincarnation and of life after death, and shamanistic contact with the spirits of the ancestors. They also include the experience of being in tune with, or being a conduit for, some power greater than ourselves, in writing, singing, painting, or suddenly seeing how an aspect of the physical world works. They include, too, a feeling of being at one with another person or with a group, being absorbed or transported by a work of art or music, or by an aspect of nature (blossom in spring-time, hills patchworked with cloud shadows, sea breakers roaring).

Many people find their spiritual experiences in crowds, and in the shared aspirations and hopes of the crowd, whether at an evangelical religious gathering or at a football match. Some people call such experiences spiritual; some do not. It is not the act or the object or the place in itself that is spiritual, it is the meaning the person attributes to it. It

is not only the music of music festivals, it is the mud and the camping and the crowds which, together with the music, can provide a
spiritual euphoria as life-enhancing and as long-lasting in its effects as
that experienced during a solitary trek. People who experience such
things always consider them important.

The question, "What do you really want out of life?" is not a
remote, misty, generalizing question; it is a very individual, personal,
immediate question, and is likely to get an emphatic, unambiguous
answer. And this answer is what guides that person spiritually. It
determines a great deal of where they put their energy, their time, and
their money; and in so far as they achieve it, it will govern how
"successful" they feel they are in life.

God

It is vital that we understand that, whenever we talk about God, we
are talking about an image we have ourselves partly created and
partly inherited from others, in whatever tradition we follow. The
image of God is always made by people. It is also always limited by
our particular human understanding, which is circumscribed by our
historical and cultural situation, our family dynamics, and the chance
encounters of our upbringing. This applies equally to the image of
God in different books of the Christian Bible (written and revised by
many people over more than 1000 years), and to the Koran (dictated
to one man at one time). People have different images depending on
their particular circumstances. This clearly is fruitful ground for
misunderstandings: same word, different meaning.

Religion

"Religion" is something more solid and clear than "spirituality". Each
religion has its own doctrines and dogmas, its own statements of
belief, its own rules and rituals, its own institutions and structures
both temporal and eternal. Each religion is a self-contained system
offering spiritual guidance, guidance towards the meaning and significance of our lives. Finding this guidance within a religion has been a
human activity at least as long as historical records exist and, like all

the other experiences patients bring to us, it requires our imagination, empathy, and a suspension of moral judgement. At the same time, religious experiences require us to make a clinical judgement about their pathology, or their creativity, within that particular person's present psychic development.

Each religion (each branch of each religion, each cult, each specificity) is one expression among many of our spiritual quest. So, Sunni Muslims have one embodiment of this quest, Shia Muslims another, Alawite Muslims another still: each may well consider the others heretics. Similarly, among Christians, with Catholics, Russian Orthodox, Methodists, Plymouth Brethren. Similarly, among Jews, with Orthodox, Reformed, Hasidic, Ultra-Orthodox. Each "gives to airy nothing / A local habitation and a name" (Shakespeare, 1967, 5:1: 16–17). Each religion or sect is, in effect, an embodiment, or an incarnation, of one kind of human spiritual aspiration.

Or perhaps each religion gives this local habitation and name to an airy "something". Although this book is not concerned with whether the notion or experience of "God" points towards "nothing" or towards "something" in terms of absolute, objective, external, incontrovertible fact, clearly it points towards "something" in the mind of the believer. The book is concerned with the human experience of believing or not believing in a "God" of whatever kind, and with how people's spiritual needs can be helped or hindered through the kind of religious beliefs they hold. It is also immediately concerned with how we, as therapists, can work with the psychological and spiritual relevance of such choices, and with belief or non-belief, so that in this area, as in all others, we can be as useful to our patients as possible.

The "local" habitation here is part of the difficulty. People get territorial about their religion. We can only believe, or not believe, in the kinds of religion which are on offer to us in the society we grow up and then live in. Early Christians, for instance, were called "atheists" because they did not share in the worship of the then culturally dominant Roman gods (Armstrong, 1993, p. 5). The "true believers" of one religion/sect/cult are often extremely intolerant of the "true believers" of another. This intolerance is expressed in language, and sometimes physically: attacks on Jewish graves, for instance, or the *fatwa* on the life of Salman Rushdie, or, in even more extreme cases, war. Religions are usually inextricably intertwined with cultural and societal traditions, and so the "otherness" of the other of a different religion is impossible to separate from the otherness of their language, culture, skin colour, political alignment, geographical position, history. The conflict in Northern Ireland illustrates this as much as do the Crusades of the twelfth to fourteenth centuries, and the ongoing armed struggles in the Middle East, where Jew and Arab fight for the survival of their land, their culture, and their religion.

Our attitudes and reactions to spirituality and religion, like those towards race and sexuality, are all fundamental ways by which we define our identity. This is just as true for someone who has no belief in a traditional formulation of God; this is then their spiritual stance, and on this no-belief they fashion what they do believe in to give their lives meaning.

Clinical practice

This "otherness" of the other of another religion (or of none) is an important clinical issue. The therapist is here working with a form of "difference" that is rarely acknowledged as such. David Roediger, an American academic, wrote a book in 1994 called *Towards the Abolition of Whiteness*. In it, he argues passionately that white people need to see themselves not as the norm, or normal, thereby seeing everyone else as somehow not quite making it, but to be as aware of themselves as "white" as they are of others as "black" or "Asian", or "Eastern", etc. This book is putting forward a similar argument with regard to religion and spirituality: that each therapist needs to become conscious of their own spiritual belief and viewpoint as relative, so that they can take in and consider the effect their patient's spiritual or religious material is having on them as they would do with any other countertransference reaction.

We need to consider spiritual and religious beliefs from a developmental, and from a teleological, perspective: that is, both what caused them to arise as they are, and also what purpose they have served, and now do serve. We might come to consider that a patient is stuck in these aspects of their development, as they might be stuck in their emotional development, and we shall then need to evaluate whether the defensive nature of the stuckness is essential to their psychic survival, or whether they would be better served by learning new ways of thinking about and experiencing their spiritual needs.

Outline of the book

The book discusses different clinical manifestations of spiritual and religious experience. The focus throughout is on the clinical application and usefulness of the theoretical positions presented, which are illustrated in each chapter with clinical vignettes.

Chapter One considers how Freud's ideas about religion and spirituality have influenced clinical practice, and how these ideas have been, and are still being, modified by later psychoanalysts. Chapter Two considers the central place in psychic health which Jung gave to spiritual concerns. It is noted that Jung regarded the Christian (and other religious) story as containing symbols for the psychic process of individuation. The development of some of Jung's ideas by later writers is considered.

Chapter Three considers the family and cultural contributions to the creation of our God-image, and the developmental stages in its formation. Chapter Four considers Winnicott's placing of religious experience in the area of transitional space, and his overturning of Freud's negative view of illusion.

Chapter Five explores our clinical response to patients' spiritual and mystical experiences. Chapter Six looks at the importance of the ego in managing the phenomena of seeing visions and hearing voices, while Chapter Seven considers the link between identification and possession, and the danger of psychosis.

Chapter Eight looks briefly at New Age spirituality and fundamentalism.

*   *   *

All the clinical material is an amalgam of experiences with different people; none represents an actual person.

CHAPTER ONE

The legacy of Freud on religion

"Religion . . . the universal obsessional neurosis of humanity"

(Freud, 1927c, p. 43)

God-the-Father and the Oedipal father

Most counsellors and psychotherapists learn during the course of their training how important Freud thought our sexuality is, and how central to human psychic development are the entanglements and the resolution of the Oedipus complex. They also pick up in passing the notion that Freud was hostile to religion. This traditional understanding of Freud, usually unexamined and simplified as pro-sex and anti-religion, continues the opposition of sexuality and religion which goes back a long way: in Judaic, Christian, and Muslim scripture, to the idea that Adam and Eve discovered their sexuality through disobeying God.

But it was, indeed, Freud who set the stage a hundred and more years ago for the marginalization of religion in a psychological understanding of human development and behaviour. Freud presented himself as thinking that religion meant belief in a God who kept the believer in an infantile state of dependence on the help and approval of an idealized father; and this is often so. Belief in such a God, he writes, is an illusion (1927c, p. 30). He writes with contempt about spirituality, referring to "philosophers" who "give the name of 'God' to some vague abstraction . . . an insubstantial shadow and no longer the mighty person of religious doctrines" (*ibid.*, p. 32). Freud assumed that "God" could always mean only an external, personal God, the super-father of our projections. He retained the idea of a transcendent God, even though it is a God we should not believe in.

We can understand that Freud, with his determinedly rational–scientific frame of mind, preferred to think about religion rather than spirituality. He preferred "order" to "irregularity" (Freud, 1930a, p. 93), and religion is orderly. When his friend Rolland, a French mystic, musician, writer, and pacifist, wrote of the "oceanic feeling" as "a sensation of 'eternity', a feeling as of something limitless, unbounded", Freud responded, "It is not easy to deal scientifically with feelings", and explained such an experience (which he could not discover in himself) by its (presumed) infantile origins: to the denial of the reality of a separation between mother and infant, a denial to which many people regress because of their lack of the "more sharply demarcated ego-feeling of maturity" (*ibid.*, pp. 64–68).

Spiritual experiences, such as those Rolland referred to, unlike religion, are ill-defined, a mysterious reaching out towards an experience of links between unlikely things, such as the physical and psychic in paranormal experiences—ghosts, synchronicity, poltergeists (in all of which Jung took considerable interest). It changes shape, like mercury, and slips through our fingers, reappearing just a little way away looking different. Freud and Jung both framed their differences in terms of their attitude towards spirituality, as well as towards the Oedipus complex. Jung thought that Freud feared "the black tide of mud . . . of occultism" which threatened to overwhelm the scientific objectivity and progress of the twentieth century (Jung, 1962, p. 173). Later Freud wrote to Jung's colleague, Maeder, that Jung's defection from psychoanalysis was so that he could steer into "the labyrinth of the mystical" (21st September 1913, cited in Shamdasani, 2003, p. 52). Both, as men of their time, saw a dichotomy between science, progress, and reason on the one hand, and spirituality, introversion, and feelings on the other. It is a split many people maintain today.

Yet, in holding on to the physical, sexual basis of the new science of psychoanalysis, Freud, in effect, set up a new religion to replace the old. Dissenters from its theories were treated as heretics: they left, or were expelled. This new religion, like the old, focuses on the father. "I cannot think," Freud wrote in 1930, "of any need in childhood as strong as the need for a father's protection" (*ibid.*, p. 72). It seems that Freud's relationship with his mother was too dangerous, in phantasy, for him to think of closeness here as an equally strong need. Jones, Freud's early biographer, emphasizes Freud's special relationship, as her first-born, with his mother—her "indisputable favourite", as Freud himself described it (Jones, 1953, p. 6). So, mother is air-brushed out of the new religion, except as a lurking, seductive danger.

Edmundson, an academic, suggests that Freud, in finding his idea of the Oedipus complex, was finding a context for his own murderous wishes towards his father, and that he was free to publish them only after his father had died of natural causes in 1896 (Edmundson, 1990, pp. 24–54). Freud presents the Oedipus complex as centred on the killing of the father and as central to psychoanalysis. He considers that religion, "like the obsessional neurosis of children . . . arose out of the Oedipus complex, out of the relation to the father" (Freud, 1927c, p. 43). It is appropriate to ask how much Freud's repudiation of the religion of his ancestors stems from his need to assert his own authority against that of his father, or of the fathers of his religion. Freud needs to kill his own idealized father-image, which he saw culturally as projected on to the concept of God. Freud extends the relevance of his concept of the Oedipus complex to include the social, cultural, and religious implications of father-murder.

Freud's own religious upbringing had various elements and he seems ambivalent about what being a Jew meant to him. His nanny, dismissed for stealing when he was two and a half, was a Catholic; presumably it was from her that Freud learnt to see gas jets, when he was aged three, as souls burning in hell (Jones, 1953, p. 14). His parents were, in the main, non-observant Jews, but Freud recorded that his father read and spoke "the holy language" of Hebrew as well as, or even better than, German. Jones asserts that Freud was brought up to know the major Jewish festivals, and says he was taught Hebrew and the Jewish scriptures at school by a teacher he admired (*ibid.*, pp. 21, 179). But a later biographer, Gay, quotes Freud as saying in 1930 that he grew up "in complete ignorance of everything that concerned Judaism" (Gay, 1988, p. 6). Freud writes in his "Auto-biographical study" that "my parents were Jews and I have remained a Jew myself" (1925d, p. 7). Yet, in a letter to Roback of 20th February 1930 (Roback had dedicated (in Hebrew) a book to Freud), Freud writes that his "education was so un-Jewish that today I cannot even read your dedication" (Freud, 1961, p. 394). However, when he was thirty-five (in 1891), his father had assumed he could read Hebrew: he gave him the family Hebrew Bible, which had the text in Hebrew and in German. In this, his father had recorded his birth, and had written in Hebrew a message including that when Freud was seven "the spirit of God began to move you to learning." His father continued,

> [The Hebrew Bible] is the Book of Books; it is the well that wise men have digged [sic] and from which lawgivers have drawn the waters of their knowledge. Thou hast seen in this Book the vision of the Almighty, thou hast heard willingly, thou hast done and hast tried to fly high upon the wings of the Holy Spirit. [cited in Jones, 1953, p. 21]

In his "Autobiographical study", Freud himself writes of "my deep engrossment in the Bible story (almost as soon as I had learnt the art of reading)" (Freud, 1925d, p. 8). This is not the Freud we have come to expect—hearing willingly the words of God, flying high upon the wings of the Holy Spirit.

Clearly, we need to see Freud's views in a personal and a cultural context. Freud was an outsider in a predominantly Christian society; he was "in the Opposition" as he put it. He was, by racial (or national) inheritance, a Jew. "At University," he writes, "I found that I was expected to feel myself inferior and an alien because I was a Jew" (Freud, 1925d, p. 9). Later, he was not accepted as part of "the estab-lishment" in Vienna, a factor in his welcoming of Jung and other Christians to the small group which became in 1910 the International Association for Psycho-Analysis. They lent Christian (i.e., main-stream) respectability to his infant science of psychoanalysis. There seems to have been tension between Freud's Jewish supporters in Vienna and these incoming Gentiles: Jones refers to "national preju-dice" in Jung's comments about the Viennese group, and to the "Jew-ish suspicion of Gentiles in general with its rarely failing expectation of anti-semitism" of some of this group (Jones, 1955, pp. 38, 48–49). This was long before the anti-semitism of Austria and Germany became legalized under the Third Reich, leading eventually to Freud's escape to England in 1938. Freud lived the damage which prejudiced religious beliefs can inflict. He had a personal stake in attacking such beliefs.

But, even for Freud, it was not so simple. At intervals throughout his long professional life, Freud wrote major papers expressing his concern about religion. Consider *Totem and Taboo* (1912–1913), *The Future of an Illusion* (1927c), *Civilization and its Discontents* (1930a), *Moses and Monotheism* (1939a). And Bettelheim, a German Jewish psychoanalyst, in his short but impressive book (*Freud and Man's Soul*, 1982), argues that the mature Freud is traduced, by his English translators, in being presented as more dogmatic, materialistic, and intellectualizing than in fact he became. Bettelheim considers that "Seele" should be translated as "soul" rather than "mind", "das Ich" as "the I" rather than "the ego", and "das Id" as "the It" rather than "the Id". Bettelheim argues that, for Freud, the soul of a man, the culture of a civilization, and the immediate emotional impact of everyday language became increasingly important.

"The system Ucs" was, for Freud, like man's soul, beyond the understanding of science and reason, and its power operates beyond their control, and Freud was fascinated also by this. He knew that there was more and more still to be discovered and understood. According to my definition of spirituality (cf. Introduction), this was Freud's spiritual quest, his search for meaning, in trying to understand the human psyche.

God as superego

For Freud, a belief in God meant inevitably a belief in a particular kind of God, the God he inveighs against. We can all of us only not believe in the image of God presented to us by our particular historical and cultural milieu. However, with Freud's image of God, the fear of failing and, therefore, of punishment inevitably comes to dominate, and so this God becomes the embodiment of an early, savage superego. In this, he is rather like the God of much of the Judaic scriptures (on the whole, this is what Christians call the Old Testament). This is a God concerned primarily with power and rules and revenge and with people fearing and obeying him, narcissistically sensitive to any slight. Clinical evidence of such an experience of God abounds.

A therapist might see his task as freeing his patient from the terrifying grip of such a God. But he might well not have the training to understand how the patient could develop another image of God. His endeavours might then focus on the patient totally giving up her belief in God.

For instance, a young woman patient felt she had to prove to herself/God that she would not let him down again. Raised as a Catholic, she had left the Church in her twenties, and felt she could not return to being a Christian now until she was "good". She had become rather obsessive in repeatedly examining her conscience, over-scrupulously (and narcissistically) focusing on every "lazy" or "selfish" thought or action. She was drawn towards some of the self-flagellation practices of the movement within the Roman Catholic Church, Opus Dei. No room for love or forgiveness here, no tolerance of failure in her strict superego projections into her God. A therapist making one kind of judgement might try to show her the undesirability of becoming a Christian again, through carefully analysing her savage superego raised to the prominence of a God. Another therapist, making another kind of judgement, might try to separate her superego projections from her understanding of God, leaving the possibility that she might come to believe in a gentler, more compassionate God. We need to be aware of how our own beliefs affect our clinical work.

The image of God as a harsh superego does untold harm, terrifying people out of their own minds, limiting their capacity to think, and so to become more fully who they are.

Clinical example: Alice—God as superego

Alice was in her mid-twenties when she was referred through her GP to a therapist in the National Health Service (NHS). Her presenting problem was her crippling anxiety and depression at her inability to hold down a job or to leave her home, where she lived with her divorced mother. Two older siblings were living independently, her brother alone and her sister married and (like their mother) with three children. Alice was the only one of her family to be religious: she had started going to her local Baptist church when she was sixteen (two years after the break-up of her parents' marriage) and her social life was now centred round her church and its activities. She prayed twice daily, and looked to God to guide her in the minutiae of her daily life, such as whether she should go to a Bible study group or spend the evening with her mother, expecting him to punish her catastrophically if she misread his intentions (got it wrong, was "selfish") or could not live up to what he expected of her.

God spoke to Alice not in an external voice, but through clear and strong internal promptings, often accompanied by an internal voice. In this way, God told her to leave one job because one of the young men was "looking at her strangely", and to leave another because one of the other young women was "bubbly and chatty and popular" and Alice could not cope with her feelings towards her, so clearly it was not the right job for her. Alice was aware that if she could not keep a job, she was unable to leave home. She did not realize that it was her superego God who was keeping her at home, so that she would not, as her father had done, "desert" her mother.

Now this was clearly a very complex situation, involving sibling rivalry, growing up, an undeveloped relationship with her now absent father, and separation anxiety between Alice and her mother, all complicated by Alice's need to be perfect. Her therapist found that no movement or change was possible in her work or home situation, no matter how much Alice consciously wanted it, because her God kept her infantile and dependent (as Freud would have expected), blocking any change. Her therapist could formulate Alice's psychic state to himself in these ways, considering that her inability to leave home, presented as not "deserting" her mother, was also about her inability to imagine a life on her own. He wondered how this was reflected in the transference relationship, and how to unblock the process of the therapy.

He decided to focus on what Alice understood by being "selfish". As this concept gradually revealed its emotional foundation in guilt at wanting a life of her own, and a terror of being responsible for herself (because, of course, she would not be perfect, but would certainly "get it wrong"), he became able to look with Alice at her expectation that her God would punish her severely, for being selfish (her mother would die if she left home) and also for being unsuccessful (compared, that is, with the "success" of her father, her mother, her brother, and her sister). He thought to himself that if she had had her father around during her crucial teenage years she might not have needed to construct a substitute for him in an ever-present, decisive God, who was prepared to take the responsibility for her success or mistakes but who appallingly exercised this responsibility through terrifying threats. An internal Alice of fourteen, appropriately uncertain and in need of guidance, and the God she had then created for herself, were a powerful combination. She was afraid her God would leave her, as her father had left her mother, if she did not bring him the presents of submission and success. She lacked an adequate adult ego.

Her therapist's increased understanding of Alice's defensive psychic structures enabled him to address in their relationship with each other the totally stuck situation she had created in the therapy also, through her fear of letting him down (by not getting better) and her fear of his leaving her (if she did get better and did not need him any more). Whatever she did, she would be punished by losing his approval and/or his presence.

It took some time for Alice to free herself from the grip of her superego God, so that she could think about living on her own without the fear of terrible reprisals. She was able to stay with her Baptist church, as the primitive savagery of her God came more from her personal history than from the doctrines she was taught there.

Obsessive–compulsive behaviour

Freud considers obsessional compulsive neurosis "as an individual religiosity and religion as a universal obsessional neurosis" (1907b, pp. 126–127). He understood obsessive practices as trying to protect from a fear, and that all religious practices are trying to protect the practitioner from their fear of the otherwise inevitable wrath of God. Clearly, some religious practices are very damaging, both to the person who feels obliged to observe them and also to others. This ranges from excessive fasting to anti-gay propaganda to suicide bombers. The religious institution might shelter such beliefs and practices, or could split, with one part accommodating them and another part denouncing them as heretical.

However, it is not always the religious practices themselves that are the problem, but the fears in the practitioner of what might happen if these are not precisely observed, as with the five pillars of Islam. The Muslim observance of Friday prayers, of prayers five times a day, of fasting during Ramadan, of giving money to those less well-off, of performing the *hajj* to Mecca: all these can be life-sustaining, life-enhancing practices, or they can be life-negating, crippling, guilt-inducing requirements to try to stave off the terrible punishments God threatens for those who are "unbelievers" (cf. *The Koran*, 5:33–37).

The link with an obsessive–compulsive personality is the fear that if the ritual is not properly performed, then something catastrophic will happen, either to the performer or to someone they love. In religious terms, God will punish them, strike them dead, condemn them to hell for eternity. This is God perceived as our primitive superego. In the Christian New Testament, the Pharisees are presented as relying on the fact that they keep God's commandments; they live or die (in this world and the next) by their obedience to these rules. They do not understand the internal imperatives of love, of wishing to do good, of trusting that their own impulses are generous and fair. So they condemn Jesus because he does follow such internal imperatives, which for him override the external forms: he healed a man on the Sabbath, reckoning healing was more important than not working in order to obey the rule (*The Bible*: Mark 2:23–28; 3:1–5).

The therapist has to make a clinical judgement: are the patient's religious practices helpful to her, or obsessive and damaging? The question becomes, how much are they governed by fear? If the therapist considers them damaging, then to think of such observances as simply one particular manifestation of obsessive–compulsive practices immediately removes the whole clinical work from a special religious context in the therapist's mind and so from the possibility of religious arguments. And although cognitive–behavioural therapy is more often the treatment of choice for extreme obsessive–compulsive behaviour, it is possible to work psychodynamically with less extreme or less total manifestations.

It is not only the patient who can be obsessively compulsive in his actions. The therapist also can get caught in behaving in a Pharisaical way herself, considering the outward rules more than the inward meaning. Is she free to think round the rules, to heal on the Sabbath? A patient might bring a present to the therapist, or want the therapist to look at a photograph, or to read a letter. The rules of the therapist's training might say she should not accept the present, should not take the photograph or the letter. But if she considers the internal meaning of these gestures, she might find that the answer could be a clinically appropriate Yes.

Post-Freudian developments

Since Freud's death, and working within his tradition, there has been a mighty band of "fundamentalists" who "believe in" the "dogma" of the Oedipus complex, and in the irrelevance of spirituality and religion to an understanding of human psychology (cf. Clark, 2009). But also there has been a steady stream of psychoanalysts who have thoughtfully considered their relevance. Winnicott's powerful contribution is considered in Chapter Four. There have also been—and notice the titles—books by psychoanalysts: *Psycho-Analysis and Zen Buddhism* (Fromm, 1960), *The Birth of the Living God* (Rizzuto, 1979), *Psychoanalysis and Religious Experience* (Meissner, 1984), *In the Beginning Was Love: Psychoanalysis and Faith* (Kristeva, 1987), *Emotion and Spirit* (Symington, 1994), *The Psychoanalytic Mystic* (Eigen, 1998). This trend is bursting into ever greater prominence, as witness the book edited by Black, an analyst from the Institute of Psychoanalysis, *Psychoanalysis and Religion in the 21st Century: Competitors or Collaborators?* (2006)—a title that would have been unthinkable ten, even five, years earlier. In this book, influential contemporary psychoanalysts are taking seriously the interface between analysis and religion and spirituality, and not only in the Judaic tradition: Buddhism and Vedanta are also considered. These writers treat spirituality and religion as observed psychic phenomena, to be understood as contributing to people's defences and aspirations, like any other.

CHAPTER TWO

Jung: the symbolic and the arcane

"The soul possesses by nature a religious function"

(Jung, 1944, par. 14)

L ike Freud, Jung also strove to get free of his father and of his father's God. In *Memories, Dreams, Reflections* (1962), we read how much he was affected by what he perceived as his clergyman father's loss of faith yet persistence in his role; the fantasy, when Jung was twelve, of God dropping a great turd from heaven on the shining roof of Basel cathedral shows what Jung's internal God thought at this time of the church of his father. We could link these two facts, and think that Jung's fantasy was a way of expressing his adolescent contempt for his father (Jung, 1962, pp. 52–56). Not surprisingly, like Freud, Jung also found much to criticize in the religion that surrounded him, at home and later.

Jung, however, was very comfortable with the breadth and intangibility of "spirituality". Spirituality, reaching out towards a vital yet indefinable goal, can include everything we call "paranormal". Jung had personal experience of such phenomena from boyhood, and as an adult. In 1916, the pressure building in Jung from his exploration of his unconscious psyche led to an experience of someone ringing the door-bell "frantically", desperate to come in, and to the feeling of huge pressure in the house, as if it was "crammed full of spirits". When he started to write what he felt, the pressure eased (*ibid.*, pp. 178–179, 215–216).

It is therefore not surprising that Jung saw all spiritual experiences as aspects of our unconscious psyche, crowding forward to enter consciousness. For him, the simple existence of a belief means it is "real" in the sense of being part of human experience, and is, therefore, to be taken seriously. "I regard the psyche as *real*", he wrote in "Answer to Job":

> If, for instance, a general belief existed that the river Rhine had at one time flowed backwards from its mouth to its source, then this belief would in itself be a fact . . . Beliefs of this kind are psychic facts which cannot be contested and need no proof. Religious statements are of this type. [Jung, 1952, par. 553; cf. par. 752]

Such an attitude in a therapist leads her to consider it as a straight-forward manifestation of the unconscious psyche when a patient talks about attending a spiritualist meeting and hoping to make contact with the dead, or going to a fortune-teller to have their palm read. It gives the therapist a theoretical framework within which to think about what the patient is saying. These are psychic facts like any other. They bring the same questions to the therapist's mind as any other: why tell me this now? What does this, as an image, signify?

Religious structure as containment

A religion can contain and express a person's spirituality. It might limit it, but also it might make it safe. In 1940, Jung wrote that by believing in a religious creed, authority, and sacred writings, "people are effectively protected against immediate religious experience", and, in 1946, he considered the world's religions as "great psychotherapeutic systems" (Jung, 1940, par. 75, 1946, par. 390). In 1935, he noted that if one of his patients was content to return to his Christian church, whether Catholic or Protestant, Jung was content to end the therapy, in the understanding that his patient had found a suitable (for that person, at that time) spiritual and psychic home (Jung, 1935, par. 21).

Clinical example: Brian/Buddhananda—religious structure as suitable containment

Brian, who took the name Buddhananda when he became a Buddhist at thirty-one, had spent a distracted, wandering youth. He seems to have felt unable, or unwilling, to meet the bright achievements his father wanted for him, and to have received no support for any other choices from his depressed, and largely unavailable, mother. Born in Australia, he began his travels when he left school. He came to Europe and stayed with distant relatives in Germany for a while, got a job, moved on, and a few years later came to England with a young English woman he had met in Italy. He decided he wanted to study and attended a Transcendental Meditation course, left his girl-friend, had various short-term relationships and short-term jobs, enrolled for a degree course in Comparative Religion and Psychology (funded by his parents), found he could not get himself to lectures or produce his assignments, left the course, and arrived as a low-fee-paying training patient for a psychotherapy trainee.

Her initial struggle was to settle him in. There were recurring difficulties about his attendance and his ability to pay his fee. Within the sessions, however, he did not drift off; he was bright and talkative and engaging. It was only after some months that his therapist realized that her experience of not really understanding what he was saying, or of feeling exhausted after a session, were reflecting Brian's fear of engaging with her on other than a superficial level—his fear of finding out that she might be useful to him and that he might come to rely on her.

In a compensatory movement towards the other pole (of engagement and dependency), Brian attended another course which led to his becoming involved in a psychological organization which had all the hallmarks of being a cult—it wanted more and more of his time and his money, and lectured him about his lack of commitment. His therapist interpreted his interest in this organization as a defence against a deeper engagement with her, and as expressing his longing to belong and to be cared for. Brian found he had to choose between attendance at a weekly group at the organization, and one of his therapy sessions. Despite pressure from Brian, and trying not to be swayed by her need for him to complete the required months of therapy for her training, his therapist held firm and did not agree to change his session time. After weeks of uncertainty, Brian eventually opted for the therapy.

However, he almost immediately began to attend a centre of the Friends of the Western Buddhist Order, at first for social events and *tai chi* classes. He gradually eased his way out of the clutches of the cult into the less demanding, more simply availably there, presence of the Buddhists. He joined a meditation group, went on a retreat, and began to meditate also at home. After a further year or so, he decided Buddhism was for him, officially joined the group, and adopted his Buddhist name of Buddhananda.

During this time, he also got a permanent job and bought some storage units for his rented flat. He began to talk of ending the therapy, and his therapist, feeling he was well held in the Buddhist community, and was settling in also to the wider community in the town, considered that he had found here the containment and the experience of belonging that he needed, as well as the opportunity to continue to explore, with discipline, the religious and spiritual ideas and ideals he had long been interested in. He had become able to make a commitment, to say to himself that he valued and wanted this thing. The therapy ended, not because it could not have developed further, but because Buddhananda had made his own choices and seemed to have found what he had been seeking when he came to therapy.

Religious story as symbolic of psychic processes

Jung often used the terms "spiritual" and "psychic" interchangeably, and thought the religions of the world were symbolic representations of a psychological process. Religious story he called "'therapeutic' myth" (Jung, 1942, par. 291). He thought, for instance, that we indeed create our image of God in our own image (from his psychological perspective, how else would we find it?), and that what we call God is a recipient of projections of our self (Jung, 1951, par. 305). This is using "self" in one of the several meanings Jung gave it at different times, as "psychic totality, consisting of both conscious and unconscious contents" (Jung, 1921, par. 789, definition added in 1960).

Therefore, "We cannot tell," he wrote, "whether God and the unconscious are two different entities" (Jung, 1952, par. 757). We use with

God the same mechanism of projection which we employ all the time with other people, situations, stories, or images, so that we can become aware (or get rid) of what is unconscious in us, such as our envy, our capacity to love, or our longing for, and fear of, dependency.

Jung understood the sign for the Tao as meaning "to go consciously, or the conscious way" and that the ancient Chinese religions were paths towards what he called individuation—the increasing integration into consciousness of more and more of our unconscious psyche (Jung, 1931, par. 28). In contrast, he thought that Christianity was deeply flawed because it did not include "the fourth", which is Satan (Jung, 1942, pars. 251–258). He thought that Christ represents only the "light" side of our self; he is "one-sidedly perfect" and needs our shadow, Satan, "to restore the balance" (Jung, 1951, pars. 76–77). Satan, thus, represents the "string of hard facts" about ourselves which we prefer not to know (Jung, 1946, par. 400). He is, therefore, ejected from an idealized version of who we are, which is unfortunately contrary to truth and therefore to psychic health. This sanitized version of our self Christians then call God.

Later Jung welcomed the new Roman Catholic dogma of the Bodily Assumption of the Blessed Virgin Mary into heaven. He believed this symbolized that at last Christianity was willing to include woman, sex, the body, the earthiness of this mortal world, into its concept of the self. (This happy potential outcome has not yet been realized.) He thought the birth of Jesus, as one among many stories of the birth of a divine child, symbolized the beginning of the individuation process in each person (Jung, 1952, pars. 748–758) and that godparents are a reminder to us that every child has unconscious, divine powers, which need to be accommodated along with the developing conscious ones (Jung, 1938[1954], par. 172).

Indeed, Jung considered the whole Christian story as a series of symbols, but all constantly available, since archetypal, or eternal, events do not follow each other in a time-bound sequence: "what happens in the life of Christ happens always and everywhere", he wrote (Jung, 1940, par. 146). This "life" is a mode of experience/being in parallel with our everyday world, to which we can gain access through the symbols of the great religions, "as if a window or a door had been opened upon that which lies beyond space and time" (Jung, 1940[1941], pars. 307, 323). The fact, which group therapists often emphasize, that we are not the only person to suffer in a particular way is, for Jung, expressed in Christian story in tremendous, emotionally intense, numinous symbols. He called them "archetypal" because of these qualities, and because they shape our experience (cf. Samuels, Shorter, & Plaut, 1986). The emotional intensity is part of the healing power of an engagement with the symbol, as clinicians experience daily in their work.

Yet, despite the advantages of being able to connect with such Christian symbolism, Jung also saw the great world religions as belief systems that people would be able to leave behind when they understood and could live by the profound psychological truths these systems represented (Jung, 1941, par. 287). In this, he saw them as continuations of the myths (about gods, heroes, men and women, animals, nature) of ancient civilizations, which he also understood as representing symbolically profound psychological processes. So, for Jung, the "myth" he lived by was the myth of individuation, not the myth of Christianity (Jung, 1962, pp. 195, 224). His spiritual aim was a fullness of life, a wholeness of personality, the integration of psychic opposites, the acknowledgement of our Shadow, and a sense of belonging to a collective process. He thought a new epoch was dawning, and that people were now called to become more fully adult and self-responsible, withdrawing more of their projections and acknowledging that both God and Satan live in their own human psyche (Jung, 1942, par. 264).

"Spiritual health", for Jung, was working towards this goal of individuation. Like Freud, he wanted everyone to believe in *his* version of a new "religion", and in 1932 could phrase it that a good therapeutic outcome was when a patient regained his "religious outlook" (Jung, 1932, par. 509).

Clinical example: Chandra—the search for spiritual meaning

Chandra was a second generation immigrant whose parents had come to Britain from their life of small-scale farming in the Punjab. She was aged thirty-five and married; her husband had also emigrated from the Punjab, in order to marry her when she was seventeen. She came to a women's therapy centre with complaints about pains in her back, about her husband, and about her poverty. Her family of origin was Hindu. She was profoundly dissatisfied with her life. She and her husband both wanted children, but in seventeen years of marriage she had not become pregnant, and they could not afford further IVF treatment. She felt that her family looked down on her because she was childless; she could not complain to them about her husband; family restrictions prevented her from working. She felt unwelcome and useless wherever she went.

She and her therapist did a great deal of work on the psychic causes of her physical pains and the purpose these served in her life, on her relationship with her husband, and how this repeated in many ways her childhood relationship with her mother, and on what being poor meant to her, financially and emotionally. The question which came to the surface with ever greater urgency became, "Who am I?": who am I if I do not have the sign and status of children, as my mother had and as my brother has and as my friends have; who am I if my husband is not the hero I had hoped he would be to rescue me from the narrowness of my parents and their family; who am I if I feel myself to be poor? Her therapist thought of her narcissism and her disappointment in the reality of her ordinary life. She thought also of Chandra's social and racial isolation. Her situation seemed one of a complex interaction between concentric circles, each imprisoning her, each defining her present misery.

The therapeutic pair stayed for what seemed a long time stuck in disappointment and in Chandra's resentment at the limitations that her life offered her. Images of death recurred in her material: memories of the deaths of her grandparents when she was the same age as her brother's children now, and of her mother's resultant incapacitating depression, increased by what she felt as her exile in England; the death of a cousin's husband, deaths in contemporary political life (the defeat of an army, the murder of refugees); deaths, particularly violent deaths, reported in the local paper. Her therapist dreaded their sessions, feeling she was witnessing a self-sustaining funeral pyre. She had identified with Chandra's helplessness and dread, killing any capacity to think outside the grave of her own hope for the therapy, of Chandra's hope of children. She could not at this time understand her feelings as countertransference, and so be able to process and use them in the work.

Then, one day, a literal bitter smell of ashes pervaded the consulting room from a neighbour's bonfire. This started a train of thought in the therapist about getting rid of what was now rubbish; she had a startlingly vivid memory of a photograph of the funerary *ghats* in Benares, then a dynamic picture of a new phoenix arising out of the ashes of its own funeral pyre, and then an association to the death and dismemberment of Osiris and the gathering together of his parts by Isis, so that he lived again, a symbol of fertility in the spring. Thinking of Jung, the therapist saw these as symbols of the resurrection to a new and at first unrecognized life from the death of the ego in an experience of failure and despair. She wondered what this new life might entail, but she felt it in herself, with a renewed energy and renewed hope in the work. She became able again to think, and to see how Chandra's stuckness was in part a defence against the risk of any new life.

The therapist began to look with Chandra at the compensatory opposite to her preoccupation with death, to consider with her that although all these things were true, they were not the whole or only truth. She now saw all Chandra's images of death as just that— images. She was freed from identifying with Chandra's experience that this is all there is. And so the work could continue along the path of individuation, along the path of Chandra's longing to find meaning and significance in her life despite her disappointments and failures.

This therapist had no religious belief but, because of her associations to the phoenix and to Osiris, she began to see the therapy in terms of a spiritual quest. She spoke of Chandra's fear of daring to want anything good, to hope that she might yet find some happiness, with the concomitant risk of further disappointment. The therapist acknowledged how much Chandra had hoped for from the therapy, and how disappointed she was that it had not made things all right. This brought to light Chandra's conscious but secret hope that the therapy would somehow release a psychic or physical block, and so enable her to have children.

Chandra's healing came, as we would expect, from internal change effected through the transference relationship. After being able to speak her mind, however shyly, to her therapist, she became able to speak more openly to her parents, and to her husband. The therapy at the women's centre had to end, because Chandra had had the allotted eighteen months. Moving out to another therapist, with the rage and mourning and initiative this entailed, led to her claiming the right to go out into the community in other ways. Conflict with her husband and family became intense, and Chandra's life became very painful; her physical pains, however, decreased in intensity. There was some violence of words and action from her husband. Eventually, after much suffering, but with a renewed, rather sad, and consciously distant relationship with him, Chandra joined an Access course at her local college, and she started to work outside the home. She went to Yoga classes. Over a long time, she became a member of a local pressure group, and eventually stood for election to the town council; she was elected, and became involved particularly in issues around social care and education for deprived and disabled children. It was a therapy of many years, but, through it, Chandra did find a meaning and a purpose for her life, did develop a great many of her own resources, and did become more fully who she potentially was.

Chandra's only expressed interest in religion or spirituality was her identification of both her parental and her husband's family with the Hindu religion, and her wish to leave both family and religion behind her. Yet, both her therapists thought of the work as a profoundly spiritual therapy.

Further understanding of religious symbols

Jung was primarily interested in the Christian story, and most subsequent analytical psychologists have come from a Judaic or Christian background. There is, therefore, often a focus on these traditions in later considerations of Jung's concept of religious story as symbolizing psychological processes. Edinger has written, in *The Christian Archetype* (1987), how the details of the Christian story illustrate the individuation process.

Other writers use other traditions. Marie von Franz, who studied with Jung, used fairy stories from all over Europe with this kind of psychological understanding, and thereby enriched their usefulness for amplification of clinical material for those who enjoy the stories anyway (von Franz, 1970, 1974). Neumann, who also studied with Jung, worked particularly with Egyptian creation stories in this way, understanding the separation of the heaven and the earth as a paradigm for the separating of consciousness from unconsciousness, of light from darkness, of the World Parents from each other, of all opposites (Neumann, 1954).

There is also a recent surge in publications by people trained in both Freudian and Jungian traditions examining the connections between depth psychology and Buddhism, such as the collections of papers edited by Molino (1998) and by Mathers, Miller, and Ando (2009). Many of these papers explore the symbolic meaning of Buddhist stories and practices.

Many counsellors and psychotherapists consider that Jung is more pro-religion than Freud, but there is an argument that Jung's comprehensive psychologizing of religion destroys it more thoroughly than does Freud's reductionism, because, for Jung, the concept of God is entirely internalized (Palmer, 1997, pp. 167, 195). What was more important for Jung, however, was his interest in, and commitment to, a spiritual way of living, of which for him religion was but one avenue. As clinicians, our sole interest in religious or spiritual material, from our patient or from our own countertransference responses, is how much it is a help or a hindrance to the patient in that particular manifestation at that particular time. We are in the business of psychic truth and psychic purposefulness.

We do not have to agree with—or even understand—some of Jung's more esoteric pronouncements: about the *pleroma*, the *unus mundus*, synchronicity, UFOs, the Bodily Assumption of the Blessed Virgin Mary into heaven, the use an Indian might make of Yoga, the meaning of *The Tibetan Book of the Dead*. Equally, Jung's wide range of reference to a plethora of ancient myths from many lands could well leave us bewildered, and his lengthy analysis of Longfellow's poem *Hiawatha* could render us, frankly, unmoved. We might not find helpful his references to alchemy, *The Tao*, or to Christianity. If these are not stories or methods of thinking we are familiar with, or mysteriously drawn to, there is no value in mastering them solely in order then to understand them symbolically. It is the patient's material we need to be willing to understand symbolically, and the other terms of reference can aid us in this task. But Jung's insistence on the constant presence of the symbolic, and his extension of symbolic thinking to include, and to explain psychologically, what had often before been taken literally in areas of spirituality and religion are invaluable tools.

The creation of our internal image of God: influences personal, developmental, and cultural

"In the course of development each individual produces an idiosyncratic and highly personalized representation of God"

(Rizzuto, 1979, p. 90)

Introduction

Many clinicians do not realize that the concept, or experience, of God has more than one expression, or image. It varies from one religion to another, within one religion in each sect, and within each sect from one person to another. Moreover, a person's individual image of God appropriately changes through developmental stages. Any image of God is, therefore, very limited and specific to that particular person at that particular time.

This lack of understanding can lead to the therapist thinking she knows what a patient means when he says, for instance, "I think God wants me to stay home and look after my mother." This is because the therapist thinks there is only one image of God, her own. So she unreflectingly distorts the patient's meaning by making his experience fit hers. What are our assumptions, our prejudices? We need to know enough to know that we do not know: we cannot know what attending weekly worship, for instance, means to this patient now, until he tells us.

What do we project, for instance, of our associations to "Eastern" or "Indian"? If a patient tells us that she goes to the Hindu temple every week with her mother, do we immediately have a picture of a limiting culture, the segregation of men and women, a young adult overly tied in to family expectations? Or do we have an exotic picture of female energy and power, coming from representations we have seen of the Great Goddess massaging her consort Siva into wakefulness and action, or of her giving birth, or of her defeating a horde of monsters in battle? Do we imagine infinite possibilities for our patient, of her identifying with one of the many female Gods, aspects of the Great Goddess, whose patronage includes speech, learning, and wealth, as well as the power to bring to life and to destroy (cf. Mookerjee, 1988, pp. 76, 44, 51, 62–63)? Do we automatically denigrate or idealize?

This chapter is intended to help the therapist to think around her own, as well as her patient's, images of God. A woman therapist who is an atheist might well not believe in the remorselessly male God of Christianity, or of Islam. To not believe in such a God can seem the only route to sanity and health. Hampson, a Christian theologian, suggests that a girl who prayed to a mother in heaven, rather than to a father, would have not only a different conception of God, but also a different sense of herself (Hampson, 1990, p. 83). The therapist's awareness of such cultural and religious factors can increase the depth of her clinical understanding.

Our image of God: one among many images in the internal world

A child of two cannot rely on her own creative capacity; she cannot credit the existence of a being which/who cannot ever be seen, unlike mummy and daddy, who come and go. Looking round the church, she asks, "Where God?" Aged three, this child can begin to imagine a being who is present but not visible, whether it is a bear under the bed or God surrounding her with love. Aged four, she can clearly distinguish between external and internal reality, saying, "I am the only real person in my bed," as she describes a dream of a ghost. Her internal objects of mother and of father begin to develop at an instinctive, preverbal stage; her internal object, or image, of God, though partly dependent on these early images, comes later.

Our image of God is exactly that: "our image". In just the same way as we can imagine "being a mother" only in the context of images of mothering we have ourselves experienced or seen around us, or read about, so we can develop our image of God only as an amalgam of our personal, family, and wider cultural experience. Like our image of mother, our image of God changes and develops through our growing-up years, and can be modified also in adult life through our experience in the external world, or it can get stuck at a particular stage, or several images of God can co-exist in us, as can several images of mother. The "mother transference" in therapy can have startlingly varied expressions, even in the same session, from an experience of warm maternal care in the sound of the therapist's voice to a terror of even being in her presence if the patient fears she has offended the therapist. Similarly, like "mother", "God" can function as a rock of stability and yet be experienced simultaneously as a will o' the wisp, tantalizing the believer on the almost invisible boundaries of faith, enticing her into increasingly dangerous psychic territory. Our patient's internal image of God is there even if the patient herself has no belief in God. We can only not believe in something we know something about. We can only not believe in the image of God which we have. Whatever this image, it can be transferred to the therapist, just as can the patient's internal image of mother.

It might, therefore, be a sign of increasing health for a patient to find she no longer believes in God, if her only previously available image of God was as a sadistic tyrant who sets impossible goals and then punishes people for failing. This does not imply that a belief in God is always unhealthy; it depends on what image of God a patient has. And, just as a patient's experience of her mother—memories of the past and the relationship in the present—often changes during therapy, as she finds in her experience of the therapist a new image of being a parent, so, similarly, she can find a new image of being a God.

Clinical example: Diana—a restricted Christian woman

In the work with Diana, we can see how both the religion and the image of God she had received as a child were reinforced by her family structures to create a prison that drove her to depression. The meshing of cultural and family influences restricted her experience of God to one of infantile dependence and fear. Her family happened to belong to a Christian sect; but a Muslim, Hindu, Sikh, or Jewish family could create a very similar environment for their daughter.

It was work in the transference that freed Diana from some of these restrictions. As she became able to imagine and to realize more of her own repressed and unconscious wishes and feelings, so her experience of God changed to accommodate the changes in her experience of her own identity.

Diana, thirty-five when she started therapy, is the middle child, with an elder and a younger brother. Her family belongs to a fundamentalist Christian sect who segregate themselves from all worldly influence, such as films, theatre, fiction. But the children usually go to mainstream schools, where, inevitably, they meet these influences. In this sect, only the men have authority in the church and in the home. It is men who preach, read the lessons, are responsible for the money and for the organization of the community, lead the groups, administer moral exhortations. At home, her father was head of the household, her mother obeying him in all matters, such as about money, clothes, education, holidays, food, how to apply the policy of segregation from the world. Diana's brothers went to grammar schools, on scholarships, but she was not allowed to sit for a scholarship on the grounds that education was less important for a girl and that there would not be enough money to support the younger brother at grammar school if he did not win a scholarship.

The image of God, then, in her religion and in her family, was of a God who supported male dominance and was afraid of, and condemned, other ways of living, especially (for women) sexual freedom and ambition (wanting things) in all its forms.

So, Diana grew up in a family and religious environment in which women were treated as less able and less important than men, and which regarded the world "outside" as evil and dangerous. She had little confidence in her own abilities, and was appalled when, at college in her mid-twenties, she felt an attraction to a man who was "an outsider". She retreated into a depression, crippling enough to prevent her from studying for the qualification which might have enabled her to get a better job and leave home. As the years went by and her biological clock ticked remorselessly on, her inability to move out into the world and her depression both increased. Her GP prescribed antidepressants, and eventually referred her for NHS therapy.

Her therapist had known nothing about this particular sect before meeting Diana, and was inexperienced, being a junior doctor on a six-month psychotherapy placement. He was appalled at what he heard, likening it in supervision to women wearing a *burqa* and walking a few steps behind their husbands, not allowed to leave home unless accompanied by a male relative. He was angry and wanted to rescue Diana, to help her to leave the sect, but his supervisor warned him to go slowly, wondering where Diana would go if she did leave. Her family structure, her moral structure, her social structure, her spiritual structure, were all located in her Christian community. Her total psychic structure, which allowed her to function in the world, was dependent on her family and on the sect.

Diana answered the supervisor's question by becoming very dependent on her once-weekly therapy, regressing to a state of incapacity and tears, which her therapist found hard to distinguish from her depression. She became unable to work at all. Her therapist became alarmed. His supervisor suggested that he could think of this primarily as Diana's wish to regress to an infantile state to avoid coping with the complexities of the outside world, which coming to therapy represented, and with the conflicts between the teachings in which she had been brought up and her own inclinations. With a terrible sense of shame and wrong-doing, Diana soon reported dreaming about her therapist: at first, a dream about her visiting his home when he was not there and going up to his bedroom, then, getting closer, about her touching him on the arm, and wearing the same colour clothes (as underwear) as the sweater he had worn the previous week. Her therapist was embarrassed. Yet, he also found Diana's sexual inexperience and helplessness appealing, partly because it made him feel, by contrast, less inexperienced as a therapist. His supervisor suggested that he consider the possibility that Diana was attracted to him sexually, and that this might indicate a growing readiness to find a sexual partner outside her parents' expectations; indeed, perhaps a moving away from an Oedipal attachment to the person, as well as to the authority, of her father. He also suggested that the therapist consider the possibility that her attraction to him and her wish to identify with him or be part of his life was an expression of her wish to be more like him. So, her therapist explored, somewhat gingerly, what about him she might like, or envy, or want for herself. And the work began to approach the terrible grief and rage for all the exploration and living she had missed during her younger life, and her conscious aspirations to be all that she fantasized about him, symbolized in the fantasy of becoming his sexual and life partner.

Unfortunately, the therapy had to end when the therapist moved on in the rotation of his training. This was traumatic for Diana, who took an overdose, and needed hospitalization for a short while. However, after six months, the psychiatrist, in consultation with the psychotherapy consultant who had originally assessed her, referred her to a group, and, after considerable difficulty in settling in, Diana stayed for the allotted two years and thus made contact with other people who, for different reasons, were also struggling in their attempts to engage comfortably with the outside world. By the time her therapy ended, Diana had left home and was in the process of detaching herself from her fundamentalist church. She was transferring her dependence to another Christian sect, attending, sometimes, an evangelical Christian church, which allowed for more emotional and imaginative freedom and which encouraged engagement in work and friendships, but also still emphasized male authority. She still needed a God who would tell her what to do, and who could also replace her therapy group as her bridge to the outside world.

Parental influences

We do not have to accept Freud's thesis, that the God-image is derived solely from the son's Oedipal relation to his father, to understand the contribution the internal parents make to a person's image of God. Family environment is clearly very important. Diana's image of God was created out of her experience of her father's dominance at home, as well as from the family's submission to the hierarchy and defensive limitations of this particular sect. Diana's God was so frightened of the effects the wider culture of society could have on her that he forbade her to go to the cinema or to the zoo, or to watch television. A child who grows up with parents who are afraid of hell will have a different image of God from a child whose parents experience God as loving. The therapist might wonder, "What was this particular patient told as a child? That God keeps an eye on you all the time because he's waiting to catch you out in wrong-doing, or because he loves you so much that he just can't take his eyes off you?"

Rizzuto, a Brazilian psychoanalyst, in her detailed studies of four psychiatric patients (1979), shows how the attributes of one parent are, often with very little change, experienced as attributes of God, and that this is so whether or not the person as an adult believes in this God or not. Thinking of the "private God" the young child has formed from his early experiences, Rizzuto writes of the child's image of God that

> like the teddy bear, he has obtained a good half of his stuffing from the primary objects the child has 'found' in his life. The other half of God's stuffing comes from the child's capacity to 'create' a God according to his needs. [Rizzuto, 1979, p. 179]

The recognizable echoes here from Winnicott are amplified in Chapter Four.

Rizzuto's conclusions are based on questionnaires as well as on sessional clinical material. From these research methods, she finds that one of her women patients had, as a girl, been endlessly blamed and criticized by her chaotic mother; she finds and believes in a God who thinks she is bad and who cannot love her. Another patient, a man who all his life sought for but failed to find the approval of his family, especially of his ambitious, authoritarian father, has an image of a God who does not hear his prayers and has never manifested to him any warmth or compassion; not surprisingly, he is an atheist.

Developmental stages in the formation of our God image

There is general agreement among later twentieth century writers that the stages of development of the image of God correspond to, and/or are profoundly affected by, the developing relation of the baby and child to both parents.

Rizzuto (1979), Fowler (1981), and Meissner (1984) have all suggested schema for the development of the God-image, Rizzuto and Meissner using a similar Freudian model of psychic development. All agree that, in Rizzuto's words,

If the God representation is not revised to keep pace with changes in self-representation, it soon becomes asynchronous and is experienced as ridiculous or irrelevant or, on the contrary, threatening or dangerous. [Rizzuto, 1979, p. 200]

It took great courage for Diana to recognize that her image of God had become dangerous to her physically, mentally, and emotionally. Revising it involved revising also her relationship to her parents and to her social milieu.

Meissner, a Jesuit and psychoanalyst, gives a more detailed theoretical sequence than Rizzuto, tracing developmental parallels between parental and God images with great clarity and subtlety (Meissner, 1984, pp. 138–146). He focuses on how adult religious experiences are affected by the way in which these earlier developmental stages have been integrated. He refers to these as "modes of religious experience". Most people have a repertoire of these "modes" and move between them in response to the varying circumstances of their lives. At the drop of a crisis, any of us can regress to an earlier mode of functioning. A "deeply regressive state", reflecting a very early mode of psychic functioning, can be experienced by the adult in "a psychotic form, issuing in delusions of total omnipotence and Godlike grandiosity . . . [or] as profound and ecstatic mystical experiences involving loss of boundaries, diffusion of the sense of self, and absorption into the divine" (cf. Chapters Five and Seven). Such experiences can alternate with experiences of God as an idealized parent or ego-ideal, to be adored as wonderful or feared as punitive. Authority can be located internally, or externally in God or in religious institutional structures (Meissner, 1984, pp. 150–157).

In young adulthood, the whole quest for meaning or for God needs to be re-formed as part of the forging of an independent identity. Fowler, an American academic specializing in developmental psychology, comments that many adults stay in the adolescent stage, bound by conformity to the pressures of the group and by a perpetual obedience to, or rebellion against, the parental internal objects (Fowler, 1981, pp. 151–173). Such people cannot cope with the fully adult responsibility of their own identity and their own lives. This was a transition Diana had not been able to make even by the end of her therapy: she was still dependent on God and her church to tell her what to do, even though her image of God had become more generous because of the change in her experience of what it meant to be a good father through her experience with her therapist.

Michael Jacobs, a British academic, comments that such "stages" of development of the God-image, and such "modes" of experiencing it, are paralleled in the development of our experience of any system which becomes the bedrock of how we make sense of being alive, whatever provides an overarching meaning in accordance with which we try to act. This would include a developing atheism, or a faith in the efficacy of history or science (Jacobs, 1993). Thus, he broadens our understanding to see the God-image as one expression of the search for meaning, as one possible expression of spirituality. People can, within any system, be fundamentalists, accepting an external authority, or become self-aware, able to critique their own position.

Cultural influences

Black emphasizes the importance of the cultural tradition in building up our image of God. He is a psychoanalyst who has attempted to answer the question "What sort of a thing is a religion?" from an object-relations point of view (Black, 1993). He has tried to show in detail how we build up our internal image of God and other religious structures, and how these differ from other internal objects. He writes,

> A religion sets out to create and maintain a world of internal objects . . . [T]hese are internal objects derived from a cultural tradition, and although they will inevitably chime or clash in many different ways with the internal objects derived from the person's own constitution and history, that is not their origin and they are in principle, and very often in practice, distinguishable from these 'personal objects'. [Black, 1993, p. 617]

Black suggests that the different God-image formed by the adherents to different religious cultures is visible in the different "fruit of the Spirit" which each religion looks for from a believer (cf. *The Bible*: Matthew 7:20; Galatians 5:22). For a Christian, he considers that the focus is on engagement with the external world, and on the cross, on suffering and redemption. For a Buddhist, he considers that there is "a comparative lack of interest in social and political action" and an acceptance that suffering is an inevitable part of human existence and not to be dwelt on (Black, 1993, p. 623). But such generalizations are always incomplete: we need to be aware of the opposite possibilities, the Christian tradition of hermits and retreats, and the Buddhist involvement in political protests, such as recently in Burma and Tibet.

Bringing our God-image up-to-date: the personal

To consider these various contributions to the creation of our God-image makes conscious "the unthought known": that a person's experience and image of God evolves if it stays age-appropriate and experience-near. However much our infantile longing for security would like the image of God to be absolute and "the same yesterday and today and forever" (*The Bible:* Hebrews, 13:8), as that part of us would like to imagine God itself to be, the reality is that this, like all the rest of the psyche, has infinite possibilities, is in a state of constant flux, and is not always in its most helpful condition for our well-being.

The developmental trajectory is as necessary for our spiritual health as are our emotional and intellectual developmental trajectories for our overall psychic health. And if we get stuck in any particular stage, and if it causes us discomfort and annoyance, then therapy can help to bring our individual spiritual awareness up-to-date, to accompany our growing maturity in other aspects of our self. This does not require in the therapist a belief in God or an adherence to a religion, but it does require self-awareness, and a psychodynamic attitude. It requires a capacity to respond appropriately to talk of "God" and "religion", through having explored thoroughly for herself the existential questions that these systems address.

To be aware of developmental changes to our own image of God, and of their significance, helps us to evaluate the potential usefulness to our patient of their current God-image. As with ways in which our patient may be relating to their detriment to an archaic parental image, so they may be with their God-image. The God-image has also been profoundly affected by, and partly created out of, their experience of their parents. Therefore, our work in the transference, which can modify their parental images, also, through this very modification, modifies also their image of God. Parents and the wider culture: the child stuffs his own individual God-teddy bear with what she takes from these two influences.

Bringing our God-image up-to-date: the collective

Not only our personal image of God, or our spiritual goals and experiences, change over time. The collective view of God also, and of spiritual goals, has changed through the millennia, not necessarily always for the better. Pathology can strike us collectively as well as individually at any time. Honouring the power of the woman and a cyclical view of human life became lost to the West during the Axial Age (ca. 800–200 BCE), in an honouring of the power of the man and a belief in unending technological progress. That is, Goddess worship was largely replaced by patriarchal monotheistic religions. Gradually, also, human sacrifice became animal sacrifice became personal sacrifice, fasting, or giving money to the poor. MacKenna, a Jungian analyst, traces the development of the God-image through the Old and New Testaments, linking this historical development with personal developmental psychological changes (MacKenna, 2002). And Armstrong, a contemporary commentator, outlines changes in different religions over millennia, in her wide-ranging book, *A History of God* (1993) (which is, of course, actually a history of our images of God).

Jung considers that society needs religious and spiritual formulations, adapted to contemporary pressures, in order to control the numinous, archetypal spells that delusional fantasies of total omniscience and omnipotence will inevitably try to impose on the individual or on society. Writing in 1946, he does not use "spellbinding" lightly (Jung, 1946, p. 196). Freud had commented optimistically, shortly before he fled Vienna for England to escape Nazi persecution, that he was fortunate in that, in earlier times, "they" would have burned him; now they only burned his books. Auschwitz proved him wrong. The power of delusions to make such omnipotent spells needs to be bound.

CHAPTER FOUR

Spirituality, and God as a transitional object

"The place where we *live*"

(Winnicott, 1971, pp. 122–129; my italics)

Winnicott and the area of religious experience

In Abram's weighty reference book, *The Language of Winnicott* (1996), there is no entry in the Index for "religion", "God" or "spirituality". Although Winnicott mentions "religion" and "God" more often than he does "spirituality", in the definition of spirituality which this monograph is using, he thought that the main task of psychoanalysis was a spiritual one. He wrote that it is "to tackle the question of *what life itself is about* . . . [A]bsence of psychoneurotic illness may be health, but it is not life . . . [T]his problem [is] one that belongs *not to psychoneurotics but to all human beings*" (Winnicott, 1967, pp. 116–117, original italics).

Psychoanalysis, Winnicott thought, needs to focus on this area, which he called "The Place where we *Live*" (Winnicott, 1971, pp. 122–129; my italics).

In considering "spirituality", there is, of course, not necessarily any image of God. And, whereas the God of all the great religions takes part in human life, or at the least has a view about human actions, the goal of a spiritual seeker is more likely to be an abstract concept—the meaning of life, love, creativity, virtue, goodness, self-fulfilment, enlightenment—or a particular kind of experience of these goals. This is precisely Winnicott's focus: on *"what life itself is about"*.

Winnicott wrote several major papers on "the third way of living (where there is cultural experience or creative playing)" (*ibid.*, p. 125). The other two "ways of living" he perceives as introversion, wholly within the person's own psyche, and extraversion, wholly relating to the external world. This third way is "the intermediate area between the subjective and that which is objectively perceived" (Winnicott, 1953, p. 3). Winnicott calls this area variously "an intermediate area of experience which is not challenged (arts, religion, etc.)", "the play area", "potential space", "the location of cultural experience", and "the place where we live" (Winnicott, 1953, p. 15, 1967, p. 126, pp. 112–121, 1971, pp. 122–129). "Live" here means to come truly alive, alive from our own self, not conforming to others' patterns and expectations.

This transitional space can be a place of rest for the adult, who will always experience "the strain of relating inner and outer reality". This is the space for play, imagination, culture, the arts, and religion. Here we can create (or find) our own image and experience of God, which is not to Winnicott an internal object in the usual sense. It is an object in this transitional space, about whom the question must never be asked: *"Did you conceive of this or was it presented to you from without?"* (Winnicott, 1953, p. 14, original italics). "[W]e agree," Winnicott writes elsewhere, "never to make the challenge to the baby: did you create this object, or did you find it conveniently lying around?" (Winnicott, 1967, p. 113). "In health," he thinks, "the infant creates what is in fact lying around waiting to be found. But in health *the object is created, not found*" (Winnicott, 1963a, p. 181, original italics). That is, it is the baby who assigns meaning to the blanket or pyjama top. To the baby, this transitional object is often the representation of a missing external good object: for example, mother when she is not there. In adult life, however, the use of this transitional space can become more complex and more symbolic, as a person engages with cultural, artistic or religious experience.

Sacred texts can be invested with great spiritual value, so that *The Koran* is never handled casually and is often wrapped in a special cloth and placed on a high shelf; the Sikh Scripture is kept in the temple on an elevated platform, hidden by curtains; the Jewish *Torah* is kept in the synagogue in a special enclosed place. A whole building is often experienced as sacred: mosque, synagogue, temple, church; and so is a common object from ordinary life: bread, wine, water, salt, a candle. These can all become transitional objects because of the meaning a person attributes to them.

In this transitional space, we can realize (externalize) something which is real already in our internal world, and in this we are creators, unique, making and finding our own true and real world. In 1968, Winnicott wrote,

> If God is a projection, even so is there a God who created me in such a way that I have the material in me for such a projection? . . . The important thing for me must be, have I got it in me to have the idea of God? [Winnicott, 1968, p. 205, cited in Abram, 1989, p. 353]

But the experience of God is also out there, waiting to be found, in the religious traditions of family, literature, music, culture, and society. Winnicott writes of "the idea of original goodness . . . being gathered together in the idea of God" as the collective act of society. He differentiates this from the fact that the individual person "continues to create and re-create God as a place to put that which is good in himself" (Winnicott, 1963b, p. 94).

Winnicott writes, "To a child who develops 'belief in' can be handed the god of the household or of the society that happens to be his". Winnicott sees no need to complete the phrase "belief in", but it seems to mean something like a combination of the capacity to trust and the capacity to imagine. A child can develop "belief in" only if he has had the experience of his own creative activity being seen as good in the transitional space between himself and his mother. This experience of his own goodness and creativity can then be "placed up in the sky . . . [and] given the name God". If the child has not had such an experience of his own goodness, any concept of God will be "objectionable or ludicrous" (*ibid.*, pp. 93–94).

A transitional object is not necessarily a thing. It can be a smell, leading us to a memory, a feeling, a semi-conscious experience that is uniquely ours. A sound can become a transitional object: the sound of the word "Om" chanted sometimes in Buddhist meditation, or the words chosen to be "sacred" by a particular religion or individually by a particular person. The sound of the therapist's voice on the answerphone can be invested with sufficient of her presence for the patient to imagine that "I spoke to you yesterday".

Clinical example: Edward—a transitional object

Towards the end of a five-year therapy, Edward was planning to emigrate to Australia in six months' time with his new wife, Estelle, whose family lived there. There were, therefore, major separations looming, both from the therapist and from all Ed's family, friends, and childhood associations to places and people and experiences: from the external reminders of his history, of his going-on being. Also at this time, Ed had left the Catholic Church in which he had been brought up and had joined the Anglican Church, because Estelle could not agree to bring up their child as a Catholic, and so they could not get married in a Catholic church or with a Catholic blessing. This issue had delayed their marriage.

Ed was already feeling bereft, and was moving towards further bereavement. He created (or found) a transitional object to help in each situation. Ed told his therapist, "You know, I can hear your voice in my head, sometimes it just happens and sometimes when I want it to. I shall still be able to hear your voice even when I'm not coming here any more." He then spoke of how he had remembered a tune played on a flute which he had heard in a hostel when he was a young adult, the first time he had climbed Snowdon. This holiday drew to itself associations from many other holidays walking in the hills with friends. He would have this tune always in mind, made rich and meaningful by these associations. He told his therapist also, in this session in which he was creating and finding ways to manage his losses, to bridge the gaps between presence and absence, that he was beginning to find the bread and the wine in the Anglican Eucharist worked for him just as the bread and the wine had in the Catholic Mass: he felt that he fed on the body and blood of Christ and that he was still nourished and strengthened spiritually as he had been before. Through this he could feel a continuity, a going-on-being for himself now with his Catholic boyhood and with his more recent past. It was clear to him that he was still worshipping the same God; there had been no betrayal of what was ultimately both true and unknown; there was no diminution in the experienced reality of the transitional object, which both reminded him of his separation but also linked him to God.

Ed's therapist said very little. She was moved by his quiet confidence and the sense she had of his stability in being able to hold on to his "objects" in his transition from one way of life to another. He had endowed his therapist's voice, the tune on the flute, and the liturgy with a meaning particular to his own experience; through holding on to the object, he could hold on to his past external, and to his present internal, experiences. And also, Ed's image of God, now he was an Anglican, was still the same image he had had as a Catholic.

The place for illusion

For Winnicott, this intermediate area is the proper place for non-pathological illusion, "that which is allowed to the infant, and which in adult life is inherent in art and religion" (Winnicott, 1953, p. 3). It is, for Winnicott, "the place where we live" most fully. Some people experience this non-pathological illusion in the imagination and symbolism of art in all its cultural forms; others may experience it through religion. Either way (or both ways, as it is for many people) such experience is what this book has defined as "spiritual" (cf. Introduction). Freud's derogatory "illusion" is, thus, transformed by Winnicott into the capacity and the opportunity for learning how to create/find, understand, and use symbols, and so to enter the freedom and expansiveness of our imagination.

Our capacity to create images (or to find them, as they move from our unconscious to our conscious psyche) is seen by many clinicians as a way we have of creating meaning. That is, our imagination, our capacity to understand events in our lives symbolically, enables us to create a narrative of meaning out of what could otherwise be experienced as a random series of things which happen to us. Schreurs, a Dutch academic and spiritual director, tells how a village was ravaged by the Nazis, and how the villagers made sense of such slaughter by telling themselves that they had done bad things and, therefore, God had punished them (Schreurs, 2002, pp. 244–247). Even if we do not much like this particular narrative, it gave the villagers a sense of purpose, and of having some say in what happened next: no longer passive victims of a mindless, irrelevant-to-them destructiveness, they became a community with sufficient importance to merit God's notice and punishment, and could earn a happier future by living better lives.

Through our imagination, then, and our capacity to symbolize and make meaning, we have some dignity in the scheme of things. To understand religious stories, of whichever belief, symbolically is to understand that our own sufferings and hopes are part of a universal human pattern, embedded in and illustrated by these stories. The frustration and despair, for instance, of our never reaching our goal can be mitigated if we understand Abraham's not being allowed to enter the Promised Land as a symbol of the historical imperative of the next generation continuing the work of their parents. Or our experience of failure can be symbolized for us in Jesus' crucifixion, with the certainty of suffering but also the hope of resurrection to a new way of life. A spiritual focus in our lives, understood as making meaning through our imagination, is dependent on our capacity to create symbols; dependent, then, on our capacity to take our "illusion" seriously. Some people who live profoundly in this way, however, do not link such experience with the word "spiritual".

Brainwashing and cults

A person who has a Judaic, Christian, or Muslim upbringing repeats hundreds and hundreds of times, "I believe in God", "God is love", "God is great", "God is one", "God has saved his people". Are they brainwashing themselves? What is the difference between brainwashing and inculcating a truth? Is it that we use the term "brain-washing" only when we disapprove of the objects which come to be believed in? Or is it the degree of coercion involved? Both seem relevant to our view of Communist re-education camps, and of Winston's "love" for Big Brother at the end of Orwell's *Nineteen Eighty-Four*.

"Mummy loves you" is also repeated hundreds and hundreds of times to a fortunate infant and young child: it is the truth, even if not the whole truth, because Mummy, after all, also hates and is afraid of her baby. But the child grows up feeling more secure, more wanted, more all right about existing and about who they are than a child who is sworn at or ignored throughout their early years. The messages we give our young influence profoundly how they feel about themselves and about the world.

But if we consider cults, and try to distinguish them from more mainstream religions, then we see that the needs of the people in authority are primary. A common pattern is: "Believe in what I tell you, and give me money/sex/obedience, and I will tell you what to do and take away your fearful doubts and anxieties." Yet, these are exactly what a Christian or Buddhist monk or nun hands over to the authority of the Order when he or she makes their vows—their money, their sexuality, and their obedience. So, a subjective judgement has to be made about the integrity and meaning of the transaction, from the side of the authority and from the side of the postulant.

In Winnicottian terms, illusion becomes damaging when it becomes absolutist and arrogant, and is imposed on others either in delusional certainty of its universal rightness or in conscious exploitation, when an adult "puts too powerful a claim on the credulity of others, forcing them to acknowledge a sharing of illusion that is not their own" (Winnicott, 1953, p. 3). Winnicott comments, "It seems that whatever is in this space that comes from someone else is persecutory material, and the baby has no means of rejecting it" (Winnicott, 1967, p. 120); neither do many adults. This transitional place then becomes a place where the person is not free to create the meaning of his own life, is not free "to live". Then illusion becomes "the hallmark of madness" (ibid.). A mainstream Christian Church, such as the Roman Catholic Church, can indulge cult-like attitudes: the generations-long cover-up of appalling sexual abuse by some of its priests, for instance, or the sadistic exercise of power in some training of novices: when Karen Armstrong was a novice nun, she was told to practise her sewing by using a sewing machine without a needle in it for weeks on end; although desperately trying to be obedient, this activity came to seem to her an attempt to destroy not a narcissistic ego, but her very self; she eventually left the Order (Armstrong, 1981, pp. 149–152). We are, here, not far from Winston's love for Big Brother. We see how the imposition on a group of the charismatic leader's particular "illusion" can lead to mass suicide, murder, or the sexual abuse of women and children. We can also think of Muslim extremists, or Loyalist groups in Northern Ireland in this way, as taking over a space in uncertain teenagers and filling it with their own violent images of God, with their own spiritual purpose.

But for some monks and nuns also, who entered their Order as young adults with good faith from both parties (the Order and the postulant), what seemed then a freely bestowed submission can come to be experienced, retrospectively, as coming from too much pressure from parents, society, or their own inner uncertainty about how to live as an adult outside a caring and responsible institution. Leaving their vows, leaving their Order, can be an appropriate act of increased maturity, as can the ending of a marriage, entered into young and left in later middle age.

Clinical example: Frank—domination by a cult

Frank was a high-functioning alcoholic, estranged from his family, earning good money in the City, with many acquaintances but no lasting friends. He came to therapy when he was forty-eight, with the presenting problem of financial worries: he had been made redundant, he was in negative equity on his stylish London flat, and had sold one of his cars. He did not tell his therapist of his drinking problem, but it was this that really concerned him—how he would find the money to pay for his alcohol. He began twice-weekly therapy.

His therapist did not offer him a reduced fee; she sensed that he was not telling her the full truth. She learned gradually that he had two further expensive cars, and several portfolios of stocks and shares, as well as money in a foreign bank account. She focused on the disparity between his presentation of himself as poor and the reality of his secret resources.

Only a year before he was born, his therapist learnt, his mother had given birth to a still-born son, knowing for the last two months of her pregnancy that the baby was dead inside her. Her pregnancy with Frank was not planned. She found it very difficult to relate to him, or care for him, and employed a series of au pairs, who looked after him adequately, but without the intense personal devotion he needed. His father worked extremely long hours, and had little patience with his mother's depression. When Frank was seven, his parents sent him to boarding school. His sister, older by four years, stayed at home.

Frank had no religious faith. He referred to God only when he angrily spat out his contempt for the boring compulsory chapel services at school and when he commented bitterly on people who believed in a powerful God but did not realize that God did not care tuppence for their suffering. The God he did not believe in—remote from human affairs, a mechanical clock-maker who set a life running and then amused himself doing something else—seemed to his therapist to stem from his experience with his parents, but she did not speak of this.

Frank did well academically, and read Law at a university away from his home town. Despite his heavy drinking and occasional bouts of drunken violence, he got his degree. His girl-friend became pregnant, but they agreed to abort the baby, and their relationship soon ended. Earning large amounts of money, spending lavishly and saving so secretively he deceived even himself, came to give meaning and purpose to Frank's life. Drinking kept him going.

He quickly formed an intense erotic attachment to his therapist, which she understood largely in terms of his longing for a mother who would satisfy him, would love him, feed him, want him with her all the time, and satisfy his physical urgencies. The therapy started in February, and Frank coped with the first break, at Easter. But the summer break proved too long, and in his regressed state brought about by the shock of redundancy and by the transference relationship, he lost his hold on his internal therapist. Winnicott writes that the baby's feeling of the mother's existence, when she is absent, lasts x minutes; if she returns in $x + y$ minutes, she can restore his internal imago. But "in x + y + z minutes the baby has become *traumatized*" and needs to mobilize primitive defences against unthinkable anxiety and the terror of disintegration (Winnicott, 1967, p. 114, original italics).

Frank, trying to bridge the summer gap, answered an advertisement for people "who want to make a difference in the world through community", and met an older man and woman, who talked in vague but uplifting ways of leading others to an experience of personal fulfilment, through providing money for accommodation and for running groups where people shared their experiences. Frank met them several times: they were charming, interested in him, encouraging. They invited him to visit one of their communal homes. Here, he noticed that the leader caressed one woman's hair, and put an arm around another's shoulders. He thought he would like to be able to treat women like that, and immediately began to imagine treating them sadistically, making them look after him in practical and sexual ways. There was a rousing religious service, with the leader preaching until the sweat poured off him, about the need to give all to the community and to God. Some people spoke in tongues, some wept. The leaders invited him to join the community, to bring all the money he had, to share with everyone, and himself to look for more lost souls to benefit from joining them.

Frank cheated. He gave them some of his money. He did not tell them how much he drank. He did not sell his flat. But he did move in to one of their houses, and he did not go to his sessions when his therapist was back after the summer. After he had missed a week and a half, with no messages, his therapist wrote to him, enquiring what was keeping him from his therapy. The letter went to his flat, and he did not call in there for a further week. He ignored it: he was having quite a sadistic relationship with a younger woman, and experiencing such power made him feel better.

However, the leader observed the relationship, and Frank was sent away. The women were for the leader alone. After a further few days, Frank contacted his therapist, desperate for some comfort. She tried to help him understand why he had found the offer from the leader and his wife so attractive, and why he had felt the need to dominate a woman at this particular time, since he had not been able to prevent her going away. She tried to address his regressed state by increasing his sessions to three times a week; she tried to address his financial state by working with his need to keep his savings intact even though this led him into debt. She hoped he would come to understand from his childhood history why he needed to present himself as helpless and yet know that he had secret, unassailable resources.

He fought for a further year against acknowledging that he drank, how much, and that it was a problem for him, but eventually this also became part of the work.

The cult had filled the space between him and his therapist, left empty when she was away for "too long". This space became filled with persecutory material against which Frank had no defences, with the illusions and beliefs, and trickery and exploitation, of the leaders of the cult.

CHAPTER FIVE

Evaluating spiritual and mystical experiences: from inspiration to addiction

"Think how it is to have a conversation with an embryo.
You might say, 'The world outside is vast and intricate.
There are wheatfields and mountain passes,
and orchards in bloom.
At night there are millions of galaxies, and in sunlight
the beauty of friends dancing at a wedding.'
You ask the embryo why he, or she, stays cooped up
in the dark with eyes closed.
Listen to the answer.
There is no 'other world.'
I only know what I've experienced.
You must be hallucinating"

(Rumi, 2004, p. 71)

Introduction

This "other world" Rumi—a thirteenth century Persian mystic and poet—describes is one which is taken seriously not only by people who value mystical or spiritual experiences but also, though very differently, by most people who have contributed to the theories of depth psychology. It is not uncommon for patients to bring an experience they call "spiritual" or "mystical", often with some puzzlement and anxiety, sometimes with pride. The clinician needs to have a theoretical context in which she can consider and evaluate the significance of what has happened.

Mystical experiences are a particular kind of spiritual experience, usually of great intensity and with a considerable, if temporary, loss of ego. James, in his seminal work *The Varieties of Religious Experience* (1902, pp. 379–382) offers four tests to define a mystical experience: it is ineffable, defying expression; it imparts an experience of having received powerful knowledge; it is transient; the subject is passive. People coming from different perspectives use different kinds of language to try to convey what this experience might be like. Rumi puts it like this:

> Now, your waterbead lets go
> and drops into the ocean,
> where it came from.
> It no longer has the form it had,
> but it's still water.
> The essence is the same. [Rumi, 2004, p. 153]

For Rumi, this is the moment of entry into the "other world", a world imagined outside time and place, and so a world at which language can only hint in images, but for which words such as "divine" and "eternal" are used, a union with God.

Rumi links this mystical experience with the experience of the unborn baby feeling safe inside her mother through the imagery he uses in the poem at the head of this chapter; he imagines the baby obstinately limiting herself to her own experience of being in the dark, perhaps through fear as well as ignorance of the huge variety of experiences which are possible in an exploration of the world external to the womb; here, an image for the "other world" of spiritual exploration. To the psychologist, the "other world" could be the world of the unconscious psyche, and the embryo an image of our narrow, huddled consciousness not wanting to experience the difficulties of coming to terms with all the multiple contradictions of our unconscious psyche. This "other world": to the embryo it is life outside the womb; to the depth psychologist it is the unconscious psyche; to the spiritual devotee it is the experience of God, of the divine, of eternal life. Gerard Manley Hopkins, for instance, imagines the "heart" of the beholder meeting "our Saviour" in the glory of a windy autumn day, with clouds of "meal-drift" moulding and melting across the skies, and when this happens, he asks, "what looks, what lips yet gave you a / Rapturous love's greeting of realer, of rounder replies?" (Hopkins, 1877, p. 31). For all, it is a more real and a richer experience than what is regularly known.

This "other world" can also refer back to the mother, to a desired (or feared) union with her. Many theorists think a baby has this experience, of being "fused" with her mother, and that this is repeated in the attempts many patients make to be "at one" with the therapist or to "get inside" her with the aim of avoiding separateness and, hence, the anxiety of not being in control, of being left, of not getting what the patient wants or feels she needs. This link with the earliest days of life finds another expression in theoretical and clinical discussions about an adult patient's wish to regress to an infantile state of being cared for, to lead a limited, unadventurous life—perhaps the impossibility for a patient of moving out from the parental home. In therapy, a patient can become stuck in a malign regression, where the satisfactions of being an irresponsible waterbead in the ocean of the therapist's care are stronger than any pull towards adult life and independence.

Theoretical and clinical perspectives

Freud, as we have seen, could not find in himself that he had ever had the "oceanic feeling" his friend Rolland was writing about and considered it as regression to an infantile state of a denial of the reality of a separation between mother and baby, because the ego was not mature enough to cope with the reality (cf. Chapter One).

Meissner, from his perspective as both psychoanalyst and Jesuit priest, warns that regression to such an early mode of psychic functioning can be experienced as "profound and ecstatic mystical" experience, or as psychotic "delusions of total omnipotence and Godlike grandiosity" (cf. Chapter Three).

Other theoreticians equate the concept of "God" with that of the unconscious psyche. Bomford, for instance, an Anglican priest well versed in psychoanalytic theory, using the theories of Matte Blanco, considers that the mystic's journey to God is the same as a psychological journey to the depths of the unconscious psyche (Bomford, 1999, p. 59). Jung also sometimes says that he can make no distinction between our unconscious psyche and God, since both are unknown, so that his "myth" of individuation, where the goal is to include more and more of the unconscious psyche in consciousness, could be thought of at the same time as a journey towards a greater and greater awareness of God (cf. Chapter Two).

Klein makes no mention of spiritual or mystical experiences, though her life's work was focused on trying to understand and codify the earliest experiences a baby has with her mother. These include projective identification, where a powerful unconscious communication from one person is received and identified with by the other. Such experiences are one way of one person "getting inside" another, which can be for various purposes, such as to relieve oneself of responsibility for the feeling projected, to communicate it to the other, or to try to control how the other responds. There are now explanations from studies in quantum physics as to how such communications might physically happen, even when people are far apart (Zohar, 1990, pp. 18–21). And neuroscience describes how the brain patterns of one person will mirror the patterns of another, which helps us to understand the other's behaviour (Knox, 2009, pp. 309–311).

Jung, throughout his life, studied the psychological meaning of his own and others' spiritual and mystical experiences (cf. Chapter Two). Winnicott also, with his emphasis on the imaginative creativity of a person's "true self", found a "place"—"the place where we *live*"—for spiritual and artistic experiences (cf. Chapter Four). In this, he links infant development with mature and vital adult life.

Bion deliberately uses the language of spiritual writers when he writes about the aim of analysis. He considers that this is to reach the area he calls O:

> I shall use the sign O to denote that which is the ultimate reality represented by terms such as ultimate reality, absolute truth, the godhead, the infinite, the thing-in-itself . . . its existence is conjectured phenomenologically . . . It is possible to be at one with it. [1970, pp. 26, 30]

Analysis, for Bion, is a venture to reach the experience of the unknowable O, what spiritual writers call a mystical experience. This can then only be understood or appreciated when it is brought into the area of K, of ego-knowing. Rowan Williams, the present Archbishop of Canterbury, similarly considers that a spiritual experience can only become transformative when it comes into contact with external reality:

> Only the body saves the soul . . . [T]he soul (whatever exactly that is) left to itself, the inner life or whatever you want to call it, is not capable of transforming itself. It needs the gifts that only the external life can deliver. [Williams, 2003, pp. 94–95]

Meltzer writes about the "aesthetic" experience as central to a baby's development. Meltzer imagines "the ordinary beautiful baby with his ordinary devoted beautiful mother" both entranced by the wonder and beauty and sensual attractiveness of the other. But the baby, he suggests, also feels overwhelmed, and needs to escape from such intensity and passion, to close down "against the dazzle of the sunrise". Meltzer links this both with Plato and his analogy of people preferring to stay in the cave and see only the shadows flickering on the wall rather than venturing outside into the full sunlight, and with Old Testament stories of Moses and New Testament stories of Jesus, as well as with the work of several poets. These links again emphasize the parallels between infantile and mature adult experiences, and between the spiritual and the artistic (Meltzer, 1988, pp. 19–29).

Bollas, writing at the same time as Meltzer, similarly melds religious tradition with psychological understanding. He considers that "the aesthetic moment" when the baby experiences the mother as a "transformational object" is the foundation for all later "wordless occasions" when, in different areas of life, we might feel "we have been in rapport with a sacred object". As with Winnicott, such sacred objects can be religious or artistic. "Such moments," Bollas writes, "feel familiar, sacred, reverential, but are fundamentally outside cognitive coherence" (Bollas, 1987, pp. 16, 31–32).

This plethora of approaches, and the entanglement of terminology, are all trying to present or describe or account for the same experience: a spiritual, mystical, aesthetic, living, real experience of a numinous quality, expressing wonder, awe, and sometimes terror. And "cognitive coherence" is just what the clinician needs when she is trying to evaluate an experience that a patient calls "spiritual" or "mystical".

Clinical example: Geraldine—a spiritual vision

Geraldine reported, after three years of twice-weekly therapy, seeing a field of ripe corn; as she leaned on the gate in the evening sunlight, the corn took on such a glow, and her concentration became so intense, that it reminded her of a passage from one of the metaphysical poets, Traherne, a seventeenth-century English priest: "The corn was Orient and Immortal Wheat, which never should be reaped, nor was ever sown. I thought it had stood from everlasting to everlasting" (1934, pp. 12–13).

As she thought about it afterwards, and since she believed in God, this experience became for her a vision of heaven, or of a world outside our time, or perhaps of her own self. She felt profoundly drawn into it. She was both very moved and very matter-of-fact about what she called her "vision"; her therapist did not detect a narcissistic pride that she was capable of such an experience. It reminded him that to see in this way is a faculty poets often have: that Wordsworth saw Peele castle bathed in a "light that never was, on sea or land, / The consecration and the Poet's dream" (1975, p. 126). He was reminded also of Winnicott, and of Bollas's writing on the "aesthetic" experience, and that this is also a spiritual experience, as suggested by Wordsworth's use of the word "consecration", implying that some other-worldly power has visited and affected our ordinary world. He noticed that both Traherne and Wordsworth (in other poems) connect such a vision with the way a child sees the world. He considered making a reductive interpretation, that this was an expression of a childhood experience revisited or longed for, but, because of Geraldine's attitude and his own countertransference ability to think about and have associations to her experience rather than being bowled over by its immensity, he talked about it with her from a teleological perspective as looking forward to the further unfolding of more of her personality. But, essentially, it remained a mystery to them both, though it was clearly a moment of compelling beauty and profound significance.

Clinical example: Harriet—a hallucinated voice

Harriet came to therapy aged forty-four with marital problems, but very soon the focus shifted to include difficulties in other relationships, notably at work. Harriet said she was looking for happiness rather than success, and she became increasingly interested in what, for her, might constitute happiness. She still attended sporadically the Methodist Church where her parents had been ardent members, but also, rather guiltily, "indulged" (as she put it) in an *ad hoc* way in a variety of practices she thought of as spiritual, such as meditation, following ley lines, and going on pilgrimages to places such as Walsingham and Lourdes.

One day, as she was waiting for her train home from work, she heard a loud male voice say, "You can't eat yesterday's fish today." She looked round, thinking she had misheard a station announcement; then she realized that this was an unembodied voice speaking, presumably to her. Slightly alarmed, she brought the incident to her therapist.

Her therapist took this experience very straightforwardly, and worked with her hearing the voice much as he would have done if she had brought a dream: garnering associations, thinking about the context in the patient's present life (external and internal, including the transference), experiencing the feeling, reaching towards the symbol. They talked about embedded habits (yesterday's fish), of thought and of action, not being necessarily good for her now, and wondered whether anything more specific was intended. The voice reminded Harriet of Sarastro in Mozart's opera, *The Magic Flute*, who magisterially puts the young couple, Tamino and Pamina, through tests to see if they are worthy to join the Brotherhood, so there seemed to be some connection to Harriet's own rather unfocused spiritual quest. Harriet then remembered she was reading a book about ancient Rome, which included information on the early Christians, their persecution, and their burial grounds in the catacombs where the sign of the fish, to represent Christ, was often used, "ichthus", the Greek for fish, having the same letters as the initial letters (in Greek) meaning Jesus/Christ/God/Son/Saviour.

This incident motivated Harriet to take her spiritual explorations more seriously, and to question whether her Methodist affiliation was "yesterday's fish" in the sense of it being her parents' spiritual path rather than her own. She began to see herself as central in her own story. The dramatic intrusion into her ordinary life did not have equally dramatic results, but eased her gently towards a more individual and convinced spiritual path.

Clinical example: Imogen—addiction

Imogen valued her spiritual experiences highly. She told her therapist early on of a couple of incidents as a teenager. In the first, aged thirteen, she had sat by a peaceful seashore, watching the waves breaking on the beach, feeling that she, like the waves, was coming to some small crescendo of feeling and then relaxing, repeating, repeating, the emotional sensation. Like the physicist Capra (1975, p. 11), she felt at one with the physical process she was watching, part of it, participating in it, her being inseparable from the being and the action of the sea. When she was a few years older, she had felt similarly, though less peacefully, feeling at one with the music she was part-playing, part-listening to: at one with the powerful rhythm, her sense of separateness lost in the harmonies and in her co-operation with other people to maintain the onward drive.

At the time of coming to therapy, aged twenty-seven, Imogen reckoned she could now access her "spiritual" experiences through taking drugs—LSD at times, and cannabis. She compared the colours and the excitement and the lost-to-herself experience of taking LSD with these earlier teenage experiences. She valued them more than anything else she did. She saw herself as "a spiritual mystic". She felt these experiences expressed her "creative side", which she wanted to find and use in working in fashion, in design, or in journalism. But while she waited to save the money and accumulate a portfolio to go on an appropriate course, she was doing office work she hated and skimmed through with as little effort and engagement as was possible.

She came to therapy hoping to find her creative side and be successful in a creative job. She lived at home with her mother, a single parent, as her father had left when she was only four. She did not give her mother any money for housekeeping. But she enjoyed her hard-drinking, high-maintenance life-style, which was not, her therapist noted, conducive to saving money to further any practical plan.

Despite coming to therapy for his help, Imogen treated her therapist with contempt, missing sessions, arriving late, often not having enough money at the end of the month to pay him, wearing either ragged, slightly smelly clothes, or seductive, tight-fitting, besequinned outfits. She ridiculed any interpretation of her drug-fuelled experiences as anything other than creative, and her therapist for not himself participating in such events. She had contempt for everything to do with the ordinary and the everyday: filling in her time-sheets at work, keeping an account of her expenses, keeping an appointments diary accurately, the time it took to get from one place to another, the ordinariness of her therapist's consulting room and clothes and accent.

Her therapist was worried about the illegality of the drugs and about the potential long-term damage to Imogen's brain. But he was also concerned at the repetitive nature of the experiences, and the fact that they seemed to him to be leading nowhere: for instance, she did not use the amazing colours she saw to suggest fabrics or patterns for clothes, or the intensity of her feelings to help with her writing. He thought she was probably using these experiences defensively, to make herself feel she was wonderful and special, when her day-to-day experience of herself was as incompetent and not in any sense creative.

One thing her therapist was sure about: he knew he was incensed at being treated with such contempt. So, starting from where he was himself emotionally, and trying not to enact a parallel contempt for her (probably her own unconscious and projected contempt for herself, despite all her bluster), he focused on her need to assert herself by non-co-operation over session times and money. He suggested that she resented being dependent on him, although she had come asking for help, that it frightened her to need a fallible, changeable, unpredictable human being. He pointed out that she felt her drugs were reliable, and that that was why she could let herself rely on them to get the experience of feeling creative. After some months, he told her that he thought she was addicted to them, since each experience was self-contained and led nowhere, so that she needed another, and then another. Such a perspective Imogen treated with disdain and anger. To her these "spiritual experiences" were expressive of the most important part of her being, and marked her out as special.

Her therapist focused mainly on the issues of their own relationship, in which Imogen did not wish to take any responsibility, linking this with her attitude to her mother and to people at work, and relating it to how much she had had to grow up when she was four, to support her mother, who was angry and bereft and herself not used to being responsible in the household.

It surprised her therapist greatly when, after about two years of therapy, Imogen told him that she had stopped taking LSD because it made her feel ill the next day and not fit for work, and at the weekend it got in the way of her going out with her mates. It cost money she wanted to spend on other things. Her therapist noticed that her clothes had become rather more ordinary, not so messy, not so glamorous, and her time-keeping for her sessions had improved. Imogen complained a great deal about the loss she felt, and about her lack of creativity. Her therapist could now explore with her how else she might experience being creative; drugs and fashion and journalism all seemed to have been jettisoned.

Imogen began to show some interest in the therapist's family, and through this she came to tell him, casually and as if it did not matter at all, that she thought having a child would express her creativity— but of course she was not going to have a child. She could not afford it, she could not bear to be tied down and lead such an ordinary life, she could not bear the idea of being committed to a man or to a child; the man would probably leave her, and she would probably leave, or be inadequate for, the child. As Imogen approached this understanding, with the grief and longing and sense of failure that it brought, she was reaching a crisis in her external life also. Her mother was planning to move to another area, and Imogen, for the first time, was contemplating living on her own. She was still taking cannabis, still in a low-paid job she despised, thinking of some sort of professional training, but not planning for it. She used the excuse of having to pay rent to say she could not afford the therapy, and she left.

As a result of the therapy, Imogen was, in many ways, more unhappy than she had been. She was now stumbling round the real difficulties of her life rather than escaping from them into her "spiritual" experiences, which had proved to be a will o' the wisp, enticing her further and further into dangerous ground. But she had not yet found her true spiritual path, or the strength and confidence to be creative in her own way.

Discussion

The sophisticated associations which Geraldine and Harriet, and their therapists, brought to help them understand the patients' experiences happen to be the associations of those particular people. But such sophistication is not necessary; what we need is the capacity to enter ordinary, everyday experiences raised to the nth degree of intensity and numinosity: mother and baby totally absorbed in each other, the ecstasy of a football crowd, thunder, the Holocaust memorial in Vienna.

Imogen had consciously tried to create her "spiritual" experiences, whereas those of Geraldine and Harriet had come unsought. But unsought visitations, particularly when they overwhelm the ego, can lead to a psychotic episode, terrifying and dangerous (see below, Chapters Six and Seven).

Techniques to develop and encourage the capacity for spiritual experiences are taught in many religious traditions. Christians, Muslims, and Buddhists all use fasting and meditation or prayer. To induce a trance-like state, the Sufi dervishes (a Muslim mystical sect) whirl around and around, one hand pointing to the heaven and one to the earth, as if they are like lightning conductors, conducting the spiritual power of heaven down to earth. Drugs are often used in religious or spiritual practice, to create an altered mental state and to remove the devotee from day-to-day cares. The incense in some Hindu and Christian worship retains something of the same effect.

Pain has often been used as a stimulant, ranging from the kind of deprivation and hardship that can be experienced on a Christian pilgrimage or on *hajj* to more severe and self-inflicted pain. In mediaeval times, groups of flagellants roamed through Europe, wild and beating themselves, and hermits often wore a hair-shirt. Nowadays, such practices are more clandestine: some members of Opus Dei, a Catholic movement made notorious in *The Da Vinci Code* (Brown, 2003), wear sharp thigh-buckles. The practices of a Hindu holy man might still include standing on one leg so that the other withers and the person cannot walk, or holding one hand clenched so that the nails grow into the palm and the hand becomes rigid and useless. We need, as therapists, to be culturally sensitive to the spiritual world our patients inhabit, but, at the same time, to have a view about the usefulness or otherwise of such self-inflicted pain and mutilation when we meet it in our patients. Is it always and only self-destructive? How do we react to the pressure from some practitioners of sado-masochistic sexuality who consider their practices to be as normally healthy as other enactments of heterosexuality and homosexuality can be?

The therapist needs to think about the meaning such techniques and such intentions have in the patient's inner world, what it is that is being enacted. But our motivation is always multi-determined: we cannot act solely from one untrammelled aspect of our psyche. The conscious motivation in religious and spiritual practices of asceticism and meditation is to set aside the clamour of the body for comfort, food, warmth, and sleep and, in so doing, to set aside the dominance of the busy ego, so as to free the psyche for union with the divine: for Rolland's "oceanic feeling", or Bollas's "aesthetic experience", or to enter Winnicott's "place where we live". But many other urgencies might also be being met: a need to punish one's self or a parental internal object, to not take in and use anything from the outside world and so have to acknowledge a need or dependence, to be special, to escape from the mundane everyday, to leave, even momentarily, ego-responsibilities which seem unfairly or impossibly onerous—urgencies very like those of Imogen. And if these are so, does the therapist consider such needs in themselves pathological, or unnecessary, or just that these are damaging or invalid ways to try to meet them?

It may be particularly hard for a therapist to make this clinical assessment if she is herself not very comfortable with her own profoundly regressed needs, and has not found adequate ways of meeting them.

As therapists, we need to consider the strength and the functioning of the ego in such situations reported to us clinically. A runner training with a group for a purpose (to raise money for charity, say) is better protected than a runner training alone to control his weight, or to constantly improve on his own time. A Christian or a Muslim fasting in Lent or Ramadan is fasting under discipline and as part of a community. These facts, like the runner training with a group, engage his ego and are likely to limit any propensity for an unconscious complex to dominate his behaviour. By engaging the ego and with the support of the structure of the group, Jung considered that formal religion acts as a safe container for the individual's mystical experiences, and Bion, similarly, sees "the institutionalizing process" of the Christian church as successfully absorbing the consequences of the eruption of a spiritual genius (such as Jesus), so that the group is not destroyed (Jung, 1940, par. 75; Bion, 1970, pp. 81–82). The structure of the community protects people from the terror of falling into the hands of the living God (*The Bible*: Hebrews, 10:31), so desired and so dreaded, of the overwhelmingly powerful direct experience of being "ecstatic" (which means "put out of place", a person "put beside himself").

As therapists, we might well be more comfortable with the presence of a moderate and moderating ego. Our time of trial comes when faced with the psychological fundamentalism of a compulsive obsessional runner or of a mystical addict. The terror of the "other" in himself or in another, the terror of being separate from and dependent on another, can lead to a compulsion to annihilate such awareness. This is the malign regression always latent in the urge to be a "waterbead" in the ocean.

No matter how alluring mystical experiences might be, how meaningful they feel, how intense and special, how refreshing in our ordinary existence, it is this ordinary existence which is the baseline of our lives. "Base" perhaps in the sense of "inferior" or "low", but also "base" in the sense of "the basis of", "the ground of", "the foundation of". Winnicott's concept of the transitional area provides a space in which we can enter this other world, and still be based in the ordinary world of time and space. Or, as Williams puts it, "Only the body saves the soul" (Williams, 2003, p. 94).

CHAPTER SIX

Evaluating spiritual and mystical experiences: the importance of the ego in seeing visions or hearing voices

"[T]he Lord called, 'Samuel! Samuel!' and he said, 'Here I am!'"

(The Bible: 1 Samuel, 3:4)

Introduction

A key clinical question within psychiatry has traditionally been whether the patient considers his or her visions and voices originate from inside or from outside. This reflects a distinction between those originating from inside as neurotic, not totally unfamiliar to our ego, and those originating from outside as psychotic.

To the psychodynamic clinician, on the other hand, the key question is how much of an ego the patient has, or how strong an integrated sense of identity, which can receive and consider the message and not be overwhelmed by it (as with Samuel at the head of this chapter: "Here *I am*"). Our task, as with all other phenomena our patients report to us, is to think about the psychological source, to try to understand the meaning of what has been seen or heard, and to evaluate its impact on the patient and on the transference relationship. The awe, the numinous quality of the experience, is part of its meaning. As with anything our patient brings us, our response cannot be judgement-free, but we have to be careful as to when our judgement enters the analytic process.

Voices/visions experienced as originating from inside

Seeing visions seems to be less commonly reported in clinical experience than is hearing voices. But, as with hearing voices, there are many semi- or peripheral experiences. A patient might say, "Something told me to", or "I felt sure this was what I had to do", or "God is calling me to do this", with no actual voice, internal or external, being heard. Similarly, a patient might describe an image, a sequence of events, or a static picture, seeing it in their imagination with great clarity but not seeing it externally; if they see it externally, this might not be a hallucination, in that they might be well aware that the scene is not there in external reality. Some patients have a gift for consciously seeing their vision outside themselves, in order to see it more clearly; this does not mean they are unbalanced, or at risk. Rather, it may demonstrate their creative, artistic potential.

Intensity of feeling usually accompanies such semi-visions, or full hallucinations. The recently bereaved, for instance, are likely to see their loved person walking down the street, waiting for them at the breakfast table, or sitting in their usual armchair. Yet, at the same time, they (usually) know that the person is dead.

Clinical example: Jim—vision experienced as originating from outside

Jim attended the Day Centre at his local psychiatric unit, and came for therapy once a week with a therapist from the psychotherapy department. He was in treatment because of severe paranoia. He was a mildly spoken man of forty-five, who had suffered severe physical abuse from close family members, had little social life now, and was overweight because of his antipsychotic medication. He suffered from claustrophobia and found it very difficult to manage with the door of the consulting room shut; the window (a high vent) had to be open.

This mild-mannered man told his therapist that he was afraid of tigers: there was much material about tigers, in story, history, dreams, pictures. Then one day he told her of going to a spiritualist meeting to try to get in touch with his dead sister, killed in a road accident when they were both children. As he spoke of his sister, it seemed he had some hope of finding in his life story a companion and some comfort. Suddenly, sweating with terror, he got to his feet, saying that he could see a tiger coming through the plaster of the wall, coming into the room.

The therapist was alarmed at what was happening. But she was afraid, not of the tiger, but of what was happening to Jim. This was exactly what Jim was really afraid of, the "tiger" feelings which were just happening to him; he had no control over them, no ability to think about them. Terror had overwhelmed him. He had needed to get rid of such feelings, and so had unconsciously externalized them in the tiger and projected them into his therapist, which she had then temporarily identified with. But Jim trusted his therapist enough to stay in the room. She was herself helped in containing her own fear, as well as Jim's, by the NHS setting: the much-used room, the knowledge of the physical size of the building and of there being other people around, other patients, other therapists, the Day Centre, the wards, nursing staff, many resources. If she had been working in her own consulting room alone at home, she might have found it more difficult to keep in touch with her own capacity to think. Here, however, acting as an auxiliary ego for Jim (that is, using her capacity to think about what these tiger feelings might signify, and why they had appeared now), his therapist was able to contain the situation until the tiger gradually faded back through the wallpaper.

It was the fact that she could think about it, and was not terrified as he was, which calmed Jim, even though, with his ego overwhelmed by his feelings, nothing she said made any sense to him. His therapist was trying to think with Jim about what aspect of himself, or of his previous experience, might be attacking him so viciously, might be trying to prevent his finding any consolation in some connection with his dead sister. She wondered (to herself) whether this was the Protector/Persecutor Kalsched describes, which was preventing Jim having any hope—"Never again!" to hope and be cruelly disappointed, as he had been when his sister died (Kalsched, 1996, p. 5). She tried to link the tiger experience happening at this time with the fact that this was the last session before the Christmas break, and that she and Jim were to be separated. She wondered with him whether he feared he was going to be eaten because he wanted to eat her to prevent her going away.

It was the tone of the therapist's voice, her continuing presence and her inner strength that prevented Jim from having a full psychotic experience in this session. It is also probable that it was because he was in a session with her that the episode was triggered: the combination of the memory of the loss of his sister with his awareness of the coming loss of his therapist for a two-week Christmas break, and the attempt to get in touch with his sister perhaps enacting a wish not to be separated from his therapist. He had also probably been able to go in search of a memory of comfort only because of the comfort he had found in their year long, once-weekly therapy sessions. So, the course of the therapy both provoked the episode, and also enabled Jim to cope with it. Jim's ego was not strong; he needed to hold on carefully to external reality. He clutched his wallet of tobacco throughout every session, reassuring himself that he had something to hold on to other than an emotional dependence on the therapist.

Yet, this dependence, which was for him so risky, was also very strong. After this particular session, his therapist was concerned that Jim would not be seeing her for two weeks, and might imagine that he had, in fact, killed her. After a telephone consultation with her supervisor, she decided to discuss with the Charge Nurse at the Day Centre provisions for Jim's care during her break.

Hearing voices: external but not psychotic

Most of the voices and visions our patients report to us do not fall so neatly into one category or the other, of inside (neurotic) or outside (psychotic). Patients frequently experience hearing voices or seeing visions which seem to come to them from outside, take them by surprise, and often lead them in a new direction. But these do not seem to be psychotic manifestations in that the patient can think about the experience and about the content, and is aware at the time that something unusual is happening. We saw this with Harriet (Chapter Five).

Such events are usually precipitated by the strength of the ego being temporarily diminished. This occurs through some sort of stress, connected perhaps with fasting/illness/some sort of bodily or mental weakness/being alone/an intensity of feeling/profound personal problems: that is, for one reason or another, the ego is detached to some degree from its usual self-affirming relationship with the external world.

When the power of the ego is temporarily lowered in these ways, contents from the unconscious psyche have more immediate access to consciousness. We could think of these as split off, or dissociated, aspects of the psyche, at the extreme, a manifestation of multiple personality disorder. But often it is more like a "sub-personality" having its say, a term introduced by the Jungian analyst Redfearn to describe our experience of ourselves as comprising many people, any of whom can, for a time, feel like "I" (Redfearn, 1985). Only when there is no receiving ego, as with Jim, is the voice "psychotic" in its usual meaning (cf. Rycroft, 1968, pp. 132–133).

The visionary tradition

Many people see visions and hear voices. Perhaps most of us do. It is difficult to tell, since people are often reluctant to acknowledge it, experiencing it as something very private which others would not understand (any more than often they do themselves) or fearing it is a sign of madness. Sometimes, it is a sign of madness, if the person's ego is not sufficient to contain and respond to the vision with some degree of choice. Different cultures and different societies in different epochs have defined differently what is "mad"—often revolutionary spiritual or political leaders are called "mad" by those who fear their influence. This happened to Jesus, and to many Russians who opposed communist ideology. One of the therapist's problems is when the patient considers as a good God what the therapist experiences as a "bad spirit", or a profoundly damaging image of God.

The clinical reporting of voices and visions need not be bewildering if the clinician is aware of their history and can think about their meaning. Such phenomena are common in the lives of holy people, as recorded in the main sacred texts over millennia. They are traditionally understood as messages from a good spirit (God) or from a bad spirit (the Devil). In ancient Hindu story, Arjuna is accompanied into battle by the Lord Krishna, much as Homer describes the Greek Gods in *The Iliad* taking sides in the Trojan war and speaking to their warriors on the battlefield (*Mahabharata*, 1999, Book 2: Chapter 4; Homer, 1950, Chapter 13, pp. 234–236). Mara, a manifestation of evil, tried to terrify the Buddha by attacking him with an army of hideous demons and later to seduce him with a vision of beautiful women, to prevent him reaching the state of enlightenment (Snelling, 1987, p. 26). Similarly, Jesus is reported to have encountered and talked with Satan in the wilderness, when he was tempted to forgo his spiritual wealth and powers in return for material ones, to live by bread rather than by every word which comes out of the mouth of God and to worship the Devil and material power rather than worshipping God (*The Bible:* Luke, 4: 1–14).

Such visions are often related to an experience of psychological development. For instance, Julian of Norwich's account of her hallucinations in 1373, when she was so ill she was expected to die, is very similar to Jung's experiences when he let himself drop into his unconscious psyche, given in detail in *The Red Book* (2009). Although Julian's were more explicitly Christian, both visionaries saw and heard physical visions, which they both considered were seminal for all their later writings (Julian, 1978, pp. 127–149; Jung, 1962, pp. 203, 207–217). Neither Julian nor Jung, nor Arjuna, the Greeks and Trojans, the Buddha, nor Jesus identified themselves with the people in the visions. They saw them as quite separate from their own psyches and from their own experience, coming from a source beyond their own lives entirely. Some commentators have written of these experiences as psychotic. But, unlike in psychosis, these people all still had the capacity to think about and to evaluate their experiences.

We might think, with some religious people, that there are beings in an eternal world which can communicate with us or, with Jung, that there is a collective unconscious or an objective psyche in which such voices or visions might have originated. Or we might attribute to the source what we have already projected of our own psyche. Then, this is what we read back into our voices and our visions.

Not only the holy see visions and hear voices. Hilary Mantel presents us, in her novel *Beyond Black* (2005), with a chilling portrait of Alison, severely sexually abused and neglected as a child, and now a medium. She, like Jung felt in his exploration of his unconscious psyche, is porous between ordinary reality and her inner world, so that in her daily living she experiences nightmare visitations by her previous abusers. In a clinical setting, she would probably be considered as suffering from borderline personality disorder, and/or dissociative personality disorder.

The experiences of Kingston, which follow, are the kinds of clinical material which a therapist is most likely to encounter outside the NHS. The question for the therapist of "external" or "internal" is less important than the question of purposefulness: of what use to the patient is this communication now?

Clinical example: Kingston—hearing voices: a non-psychotic external voice of God

When he was thirty-five, Kingston began repeatedly to hear a voice, particularly when he was getting up in the morning or going to bed, at transitional, liminal times, when he was changing from one set of clothes to another, from one aspect of living to another. The voice was external to him and male. He attributed it to his God. It told him that his punishment for using pornography to aid his imagination when he masturbated was that he would never have a sexual relationship with a woman, and would never have a child, when his greatest longing was to be married and to have a child to whom he could be the kind parent he had not himself experienced. His father had left home shortly after the family had arrived from Jamaica, when Kingston was only two, and his mother had then had more children by different fathers. Hearing the voice brought Kingston into therapy; he thought he was going mad, and it focused for him his generalized mood of depression and self-blame which was blighting his life in every respect. His therapist did not consider that Kingston's image of God was helpful to him. It alerted her to the possibility of a very harsh superego, developed perhaps from early childhood experiences, or attributable to Kingston's need not to be "better" than his own father. But Kingston had sufficient ego to use the experience creatively by entering therapy, which brought his image of God to scrutiny, and brought him into relationship with a woman (his therapist). This brought him out of the isolation and loneliness which represented a large part of his difficulties, and with the therapy came the possibility of change.

The meaning of the vision or the voice

If the patient hears a voice clearly giving a message, one area of focus is on who is speaking. When Mary heard the angel Gabriel announcing that she, unmarried, was to give birth to God's son, or when the prophet Muhammad received the *suhras* of *The Koran* at dictation from the same archangel, then, clearly, their conviction as to the voice coming from the trusted messenger of a trusted God is all important in how they responded to the message. Arjuna, listening to Krishna on the field of battle, in the *Mahabharata*, accepts the instruction because he accepts the God. But even if the patient experiences the voice as coming from their God, as we have seen, "God" can mean many different things; and when a patient hears accurately the voice of a cruel, accusatory, punishing God, as did Kingston, it is likely to be the therapist's task to question, not the existence of this God, because his existence for the patient is all too clear, but his origins, his legitimacy, and his value.

Clinical example: Len—confusion between reality/memory/fantasy/dream/hallucination

Len posed many problems for his therapist. They all centred round her difficulty in understanding, in what he told her, what was external fact, what was a memory, what a dream, what a fantasy, what a hallucination. She considered that probably she would describe him as having a borderline psychic structure (that is, on the border between neurotic and psychotic), and she wondered if he were, or could readily become, psychotic. Certainly his ego was barely strong enough to hold his psyche and his life together.

Len, aged forty-five, was referred by a psychiatric nurse at the NHS Day Centre, which he had been attending for a couple of years. He was due to be discharged. He had been unemployed for many years, and his therapist experienced him as deeply paranoid and with a very fragile and permeable ego. In a very early session, he told her of an experience he had had one evening at Glastonbury—not at the festival. He had entered the ruined church and had seen a great light at the Eastern end, dazzling him. Drawn irresistibly towards it, he heard a voice saying, "No nearer!" Obediently, he stopped. Perhaps he lost consciousness. When he dared to look up again, the light had gone. He left, and returned to where he was camping on his own.

His therapist wondered whether he was telling her about an actual hallucinatory experience or a recent dream, perhaps triggered by the start of the therapy, or whether it was a fantasy, a story he told himself, and, if so, when he had created it. Len was unable to help her to clarify this, because he was so overwhelmed by the renewal of the experience in telling it to her that he could not think about it. It just was, and he was convinced of its significance.

His therapist remembered Bion's suggestion that people who live in a psychotic world, divorced from external reality as most of us perceive it, cannot distinguish between daytime hallucinations and night-time dreams (Bion, 1958, p. 78). But there were some indications that Len had, a few years previously, cycled along the Ridgeway to Glastonbury, and his therapist thought that probably he was telling her of a hallucination or a vision. Certainly, he was giving it value as a profound and beneficial spiritual experience. The value seemed to be for him in having seen the great light, in the East, as a sign of hope. His therapist thought of the star in the East when Jesus was born, and of Jung's writing about the coming of Jesus symbolizing the coming of light and of consciousness (cf. *The Bible:* John, 1: 7–9; Jung, 1941, par. 284, 1942, par. 259, 1952, par. 740). Was this perhaps what Len hoped for from the therapy, an increase in his conscious awareness of the feelings which, in his unconscious psyche, generated paranoid terror and violence? Or was it a more general hope, the hope of a new beginning? And why was he telling her this now? Was she the great light? Was he telling her of this because of the danger he felt in his attraction to her? His mother had abused him sexually, so it would be for him a natural mixture of feelings. Or was it more to do with his total psychic state, the attraction and the danger of becoming more conscious, more enlightened, as to what his real grievances, and his real powers, were?

Len managed to leave much of his confusion and uncertainty and fear and hope with his therapist. Because he could not think about any of these issues with her, he created in her, through projective identification, the parent who would take total responsibility for the helpless infant. His therapist could think of this account as a gift, or as an attack. She wondered whether it was wise to work with him at all, whether psychoanalytic psychotherapy would reveal too much of his unconscious self, and whether his ego would be able to cope, whether, indeed, her ego would be able to cope; so, before she agreed to continue to see him, she took this session to supervision.

Her supervisor was encouraged by the possibility of ego functioning represented by the fact that something in him had known what would be too much, and had said, "No nearer!" Together, she and her supervisor decided that once-weekly work would allow Len to proceed slowly; the therapist remained in touch with the Day Centre in case she needed psychiatric help, and she took her work regularly to supervision.

She treated Len's defences very carefully and with respect, and concentrated on helping him to build some ego strength and as strong a contact with reality as possible, round the time and place boundaries of the session, and through his memories of his traumatic childhood. Cautiously, after about a year, she increased his sessions to two. As Len got more in touch with his fury against both his parents, and people at school who had also abused him, the therapy reached a dangerous stage: he spoke of hiding behind a particular fence which had a slat missing, and through this gap shooting people on the local High Street. He could locate this broken fence; he told his therapist where it was, and what view it gave him of shops and shoppers. He described it as if he had been there, watching. Again, his therapist could not tell whether these were dreams, or visions, or fantasies, or plans. She thought he did not have a gun, but could not be sure. She interpreted in the transference that she had the freedom to shop and spend money, to leave him for her breaks, to indulge herself in what she wanted to do regardless of its effect on him, and that in these ways he felt she repeated the abuse he had suffered. After several fraught weeks, the crisis passed.

Whatever she wore, he also experienced her as heart-stoppingly, shamelessly, cruelly seductive. He always paid in cash, because he liked the look of greed he saw on her face; and he imagined/experienced that when she counted the money he gave her she was fingering his penis. He had literal fights with his son. He crashed his car.

The enactments, and the confusion of fantasy and reality, were hard for them both to live through. The therapist consistently tried to establish who was who, what the projections were, what was external, and what was internal, reality. At times, she was caught up in the paranoia and the indescribable mess, unable to keep it distinct from her own private life. She became, at times, very afraid, not of what Len would do to her (he was careful with his rage) but of what he might enact with other people outside the therapy; she was caught in ethical dilemmas of responsibility as to whether she should inform anyone of what he was saying (cf. Brown & Stobart, 2008, pp. 73–81).

But gradually, through the therapist's repeated painstaking attempts at clarification, Len did approach some light, not the great light of his vision, but a more manageable, less grandiose light. The tone of the sessions became calmer. It became clearer what was external fact and what was dream. Fantasy and hallucination seemed to be less frequent. Len made contact with his brother again after many years of not speaking; his son got a job, though he himself did not. Eventually, he moved with his wife to another town, a literal new beginning which did also symbolize some hope.

Such work is very demanding because the patient's ego is not sufficiently separate from the unconscious contents, which burst through into consciousness as memory, dream, fantasy, or hallucination. But Len was not possessed, as is Malcolm in the next chapter. There was always a Len, however indistinct, who was trying to communicate with his therapist and whom his therapist, however uncertainly, could try to address.

CHAPTER SEVEN

Evaluating spiritual and mystical experiences: from identification to possession—myths of the hero/saviour and of the Devil

"The Lord said to Satan, 'Where have you come from?' Satan answered the Lord, 'From going to and fro on the earth, and from walking up and down on it.'"

(The Bible: Job, 1:7)

Introduction

We sometimes identify our ego with one aspect of our personality. In some cases, this can lead to a trance-like state of contemplation. A man reported to his therapist what he called "a religious experience" in looking at Michelangelo's statues of "The Sleepers", four separate large stone blocks, each with a man's form partly carved out of it (or being found within it). As he saw them, each man seems to be partly imprisoned in the stone, partly struggling to wake up or to get free. The statues are sometimes also called "The Prisoners". It is not known whether they are unfinished, or whether their unresolved state is what Michelangelo had intended. The therapist thought that this man had seen his own struggle to become conscious externalized in the statues, and had entered an "out of time" state of profound self-contemplation. He was woken from his trance by an attendant telling him the gallery was about to close.

More frequently, such identifications can lead to behaviours which are very difficult to shift; we become used to enacting, for instance, the hero, the rescuer, the saviour, or, alternatively, the victim, the ill person, the deprived one. Often, we switch from one to the other, but each, when it is operative, excludes its opposite. Usually, though, even in this identification, there is some ego functioning separate from the identification with the hero/victim; the person can also think and behave in other ways in other areas of their life. We could think of this as part of the ego being "possessed by" the unconscious archetype (or the sub-personality). "Identifying with" is more a willing activity of the ego, whereas in "being possessed by", the ego is passive, the unconscious archetype having the dynamic energy. There is a continuum between the two, one segueing seamlessly into the other.

And sometimes, the ego is swallowed up totally by the archetype. Then, we can say clearly that the person is "possessed". There is no separate ego, no capacity to evaluate the experience of "being" the hero. This can lead to what Harlow, a forensic psychiatrist and Jungian analyst, calls "malign individuation" (1996). In extreme cases, a person may try to reach a spiritual goal through means which are severely damaging to himself or to others: through murdering his parents to free the world from the devil, for instance, or dancing naked in a shopping centre to express the claiming of an inner freedom. Such possession by the hero/God archetype can be a short-lived experience, or it can last for days, or years. Antipsychotic medication can usually ring-fence the ego so that it has time to re-establish itself as the centre of the person's identity.

Collective action can also express a similar possession, such as the intention to "purify the race" (in a God-like way, to get rid of all human evil, or badness, or inferiority). This has occurred in acts of genocide, such as in Nazi practices or in the abducting of Aboriginal children from their parents in mid twentieth-century Australia and giving them to white foster parents, so that the Aboriginal culture and identity (seen as bad, degenerate, and perverse by some white settlers) would die out. At such times, there is still a collective ego functioning to attend to all other matters; only in the area which has been taken over is there no capacity for objective, self-examining thought. With regard to less extreme issues, this happens to all societies and to us all as individuals: we become collectively possessed by the need to build up armaments to strengthen our defence capacity, or individually to keep germs at bay by cleaning our toilets twice a day, or to keep chaos at bay by ordering our outstanding tasks into lists.

Clinical example: Malcolm—possession

Malcolm's breakdown illustrates the distinction Bion makes between a healthy mystical episode and a more psychotic one. In psychosis, Bion says, the meaning of certain actions and events becomes "a private communication made by God (or Devil or Fate)". It is not part of the "constant conjunction" of meaning agreed by a public community (Bion, 1970, p. 65). This reminds us of Black's writing about how much a person can manipulate for his or her own purposes a universal image of God (Black, 1993, p. 622).

Malcolm had based his identity on being a successful man, meeting the expectations his father had had for him. There was no room in this one-sided identification with the hero for the experience of not succeeding, not being at the top of the ladder, not being the most loved, the most wanted, the most lauded. His work, his wife, and his son all also bore this need for success projected on to them—they were all, for Malcolm, self-objects. So he had to be a high achiever at work, his wife had to be beautiful and loving, and his son had to be successful, much the same weight of expectation he had carried from his own father.

So, when this idealized version of who he was began to unravel, Malcolm had no alternative, more ordinary, acceptable view of himself to fall back on. And his ego could not adjust to the experience of partial failure.

Malcolm was forty-six, and had been in once-weekly therapy for two years. He had originally presented with a problem in his marriage: he had recently discovered that his wife had had an affair a year before. It seemed that this blow to his self-esteem led him to look for a compensatory boost. He began to campaign vigorously against a proposal to build an out-of-town supermarket two miles away from his small-town High Street. With his legal expertise, he became the leader of the campaign, and worked long hours, spoke at many meetings, and wrote many letters, gathering a lot of support. He successfully won a reconsideration of the planning permission. He and his wife seemed to have been reconciled, and he was talking of ending the therapy. But then he was not offered the partnership in his law firm that he had been expecting, and at the same time his son failed to get into university, and was living at home, dissatisfied and depressed. His uncertainty about his wife's faithfulness returned.

In response to these crises, he took up the cause of the campaign with compulsive energy; he could not stop working, could not stop thinking about the campaign, phoning people even during the night, and drafting more and more complex documents. His brain was buzzing, his body wired up. He was so tense he could not digest food easily, and did not know he was tired until he crashed with exhaustion.

His therapist was concerned about him, but did not recognize the signs of manic activity, so she hoped that if he would stop and rest he would recover. He had no history of bi-polar illness. She tried to bring his frenzied activity to a more moderate level, and help him dis-identify with his son, and she consulted her supervisor. He suggested she persuade Malcolm to contact his GP. Unfortunately, Malcolm refused. She interpreted in the transference about his not winning a partnership with her, and about her unfaithfulness to him with other people, but increasingly she realized that she could not reach his thinking capacity. She was considering contacting the GP herself, a step Malcolm had given permission for at their initial meeting. But she could not believe his psychic state would deteriorate so quickly.

Malcolm missed a session. His therapist was concerned because of his exhausted, over-busy state, but decided to wait another week. She thought later that her delaying was an unconscious identification with a saviour therapist who did not need any further help. But, when Malcolm missed a further session, she wrote to him. His wife, Marian, then phoned her, having shown the letter to Malcolm and Malcolm having thrown it back at her for her to deal with. Marian told her that in the week of the first missed session, Marian had noticed that Malcolm was more preoccupied, more tense, eating and sleeping less, and working more than was usual for him.

Then, one morning, only five days later, Marian had found him crouching in a corner of their living room, covering his face in terror and crying out that the Devil was coming to get him in order to stop his campaign: a traditional Devil out of Hieronymus Bosch with cloven feet, a forked tail, and a pitchfork, a truly terrifying figure, cornering him in his own home. Marian had contacted their GP, and Malcolm had been admitted urgently to his local psychiatric hospital.

His therapist phoned the GP, who suggested she phone the psychiatrist who had put Malcolm on medication; by this time Malcom had been discharged from hospital and was at home, though not able to go to work. The psychiatrist passed her on to the key worker, a community mental health nurse. From this man, and later from Malcolm himself, she learnt that during the week of his first missed session, Malcom had begun to hallucinate voices as he travelled to work, encouraging him in his project. He thought the town councillors corrupt and in the pay of the supermarket. He now heard messages of encouragement from programmes on the car radio, and on television. Any programme about food, or money, he saw as direct references to his campaign. This development accelerated rapidly; within a few days he thought everything that was broadcast was a coded reference to his situation, which only he could understand. He equated saving the local High Street shops with saving the country's food supplies, and then with saving the world from the effects of climate change. He imagined blowing up the Town Hall and killing the councillors who seemed to incarnate the Devil.

It was a confused Malcolm and a humbled therapist who met again a couple of months later. His therapist understood more deeply than she had done before how profoundly Malcolm had first identified with, and then become possessed by, the image of a successful man—successful in his marriage, successful in his child, and successful in his work. When this image was attacked by the threefold reality of events, his psyche took an extreme form of trying to reinstate it through the campaign, but this was not enough to keep his terrible experience of having been destroyed from being enacted in his delusions. The therapy continued for many years, to free him from the persecutory expectations of his internal father, who wanted Malcolm to be all that he had himself been unable to achieve. His wife, who had also had much invested in him as successful, left him. The sadness and disillusion Malcolm experienced as he reconciled himself to being a more ordinary man was hard for both him and his therapist to suffer, her experience compounded by her need to realize her own shortcomings in the work. Both needed a shift in perspective to see themselves as ordinarily human, liable to mistakes and imperfections, but with a self separate both from such mistakes and from the attitudes and actions of those around them.

Neither Malcolm nor his therapist saw this work as in any way spiritual, despite his encounter with the Devil. Yet, from another perspective, it was also profoundly so: offering a new way for Malcolm to live, with different goals and values which were more realistic, offering him a new self-knowledge, bitter, but true.

Identification with the saviour or narcissistic omnipotence

The far end of the continuum of identification with the saviour complex is often seen in Christian culture as an identification with Jesus. As his mania increased, Malcolm became possessed by his saviour complex, and was having psychotic delusions that it was up to him to defeat the Devil and save the world. Although he did not talk about Jesus, his delusions were of the grandeur and intensity of a saviour-Messiah. Particularly in someone suffering from bi-polar disorder or from paranoid schizophrenia, the Devil may be seen as incarnated in parents, or in a casual bystander, and the "saviour" may try to kill these people, thinking he is thereby killing the Devil and freeing the whole world. The person's psyche is split, all the bad destructive and self-destructive aspects projected into "the Devil", and the ego overwhelmed by the "saviour" internal object. Because the splitting is total, the only images which will serve to hold the projections are absolute—total good or total evil. The deities or devils of the patient's culture are more ready for this role than his merely personal internal objects.

If the "saviour" complex is not activated or, as with Malcolm, is challenged by reality, the person can become a victim of the Devil, who then has all the power, and who is often experienced as trying to annihilate him. Entering Rumi's "other world" in such a psychic state involves the horror of experiencing the Devil whispering in the sufferer's ear, "You are damned, you want your mother, you've wet yourself again, remember what you did in the garden shed", appalling, non-stop abuse. It is clear that the strain on the person's psyche is enormous, the grandiosity and the corresponding terror more than their ego can manage. Unless we are working in a hospital, we shall encounter such florid symptoms only when a patient has this particular kind of breakdown while we are working with them, as did Malcolm, and then psychiatric referral is essential.

But, equally, we cannot know when a saviour fantasy (or phantasy) underlies an action which indeed results in doing a great deal of good. (The spelling *"phantasy"* is a useful way of distinguishing unconscious "phantasies" from "fantasies", which are conscious.) Albert Schweitzer did save many people's lives through the hospital he built in the then French Congo. Ghandi did save Indians from British rule. Schindler did save many Jews from death in the concentration camps. Some people have an idea and start an organization which can do much good for many people for generations, such as Amnesty International, the Samaritans, or Oxfam. These usually start as small, personal actions, which evolve only later into a more large-scale vision and an organization requiring actions by many people.

Counterbalancing such facts, we need to remember the many psychopathic dictators who have reckoned that their view of the world was the only and absolutely right one, and that their mission was to save their country, or the world. To them, people who were not heterosexual Aryans, or who were not Communists, or who were in some other way dissidents or of the "wrong" race or colour, were seen as not fully human, and to be enslaved or exterminated. Their vision seems often to have started as large-scale and grandiose. It is the absolutist, one-sided destructive narcissism, and the need for personal power, which are warning signs (cf. Robinson & Fuller, 2003, pp. 31–41).

In our patients, such pathology is likely to manifest in an overwhelming need to control their situations and other people in their lives. So, the hero becomes the obsessive–compulsive perfectionist, who is convinced that if only he can check and double check and do everything himself, then the firm or the family will be all right. The unconscious compensatory opposite is the phantasy of having a damaging effect on other people, or of being worth nothing, or of being helpless. This may be projected on to the hero's "victims", or the person may identify with this "bad" part and see themselves as always the victim, always unloved, always irresponsible, always at fault. To have such an identification challenged (by the prospect of not being in debt, for instance, or of being valued by the therapist) can provoke a very similar reaction to the failure of the saviour myth: they do not know any more who they are.

The saviour pathology is often semi-humanized into "hero" phantasies. Heroes in ancient story have usually been half God. Jesus, born of a union between mortal mother and God father, is one of a succession of such half-God heroes in Hindu, Greek, and Persian mythology. In contemporary stories, we find heroes such as Batman and Spiderman, mortal men but with seemingly supernatural powers. Despite the many Goddesses and demi-Goddesses in Ancient Greek mythology, this tradition has not evolved in Western religions or cultures. However, we are currently very likely to meet an over-identification with the hero/saviour in women patients, particularly in their role as mothers.

Clinical example: Nina—identification

Nina was married, aged forty-nine, with three children in their teens. She was an evangelical Christian. She had gone back to work as a social worker when her youngest child went to school, and had recently started a counselling course, for which she had to be in therapy herself. Reluctantly, and not seeing that she needed any sort of help, she turned up for her once-weekly sessions with considerable resentment and bewilderment. She just knew that with God's help she could manage life on her own.

She made a great many lists of things she had to do, and became very anxious (sleeplessly so) at the need to fit in the children's journeys to school and their many out of school activities with her own working schedule and her need to run her house. But provided prayers were said every day, the toilets were cleaned every day, the towels washed every day, the house dusted every day, then everything would be all right. She could not go to bed until everyone was home. If her husband was home, she could not delegate to him the responsibility of waiting up for the last child; if he was out at a work function, she had to wait up for him. It was her vigilance, her preparedness, which, in her phantasy, kept everyone safe. When her husband flew abroad on business, or when her children went away on a school trip, she became desperate that they were beyond her help. She prayed even harder, since, if she was not there, knowing their comings and goings, in her imagination they were not safe. In her phantasy, she controlled her God through her prayers—if she did this and this, then God would have to do that and that. She did not trust her God; it was her own exertions which compelled him to keep her and her family safe.

She was the omnipotent hero, keeping everyone alive, and, not surprisingly, she found such responsibility very worrying and very exhausting. She was terrified that if she "sinned", her soul would be forfeit to the Devil and she would go to hell. This was her church's teaching. God's support for her was dependent on her placating him and being "good".

Her therapist could not ignore Nina's references to her God and her Devil, but he was troubled as to how to respond. He had himself no belief in either, and privately thought Nina would be much better off without them. But he could understand that her relationship with her God externalized and personified her need for help and the measures she had to take to try to obtain it, and that her relationship with her Devil externalized and personified the catastrophic imagined consequences of her not managing everything, her fears about the dangers of the world, other people, and her own unconscious feelings. And he found he had to use her terminology, her frame of reference, if she was to understand and accept anything he said. Fortunately, he did not need to try to impose on her his own language or belief system, and so, by not trying to control her, he avoided an unhelpful power struggle between them.

So, although he worked mainly with the ordinary reality of the external events in Nina's life and in the therapy, he phrased his understanding in terms of her need to placate an untrustworthy, demanding God (parent/therapist). But Nina's need to be in control was greater than her need to please him; she risked his displeasure by trying to get in control of his comings and goings. She asked if the session time could be five minutes later to make it easier for her to come after work, and, when he refused, she was consistently five minutes late so that the session did, in fact, start at her time, not his. She frequently missed the last session before, or the first after, a break, or said she had to take her holiday breaks at times different from his, to fit in with her family and work commitments. Her therapist's remaining attentive to her and not retaliating throughout this aggressive demonstration of her non-dependence on him led her prayers to her God to become less frightened and insistent. However, she found increasingly that she was not in control of how she felt or of what she said in any particular session, and this frightened her very much. She kept her make-up on, did not cry so that her mascara would not run, and barely managed to survive her required year of therapy.

Her therapist thought she might well leave at the end of the year, as she repeatedly said she was going to. But she failed her end of year essay, and consequently could not get a placement as a trainee counsellor. These setbacks roused a panic in her. Her therapist let her know that he understood the terror which underlay her tremendous need to stay in control in myriad different ways. This understanding, to which she responded, led her to stay on, with some bravado that it would be only until she had rewritten her essay and got her placement. She could not acknowledge any need of the therapy, or any dependency.

However, she did stay on in the therapy. She had found that she now dusted the house only twice a week, and that she no longer felt sick with anxiety if her husband did not phone at exactly the time he had thought he would be through customs on arrival at Frankfurt. Inexplicably to her, she felt a bit more comfortable, a bit more relaxed, a bit more at ease. Her therapist did not yet suggest that this might be because she was finding she could rely on him to some extent, and that this was a tremendous relief, not to feel that she was the sole prop for her whole world. He never addressed her religious beliefs directly, but he noted silently that in parallel with her relationship with him she became able to trust her God more and needed to control him less. She even began to be interested in why she had such strong reactions to people's absences, or to cleanliness and regularity. She stayed in therapy for some years, experiencing, long before she understood why, an increasing freedom.

The Devil

It was clear to her therapist that the power of the Devil was ever-present to Nina: unless she controlled her God and so made everything safe for those she loved, the Devil would punish her for her lack of enthusiasm or devotion to God. Chaos, illness, death were kept at bay only by her strenuous efforts. Her therapist thought wryly that there was not much to choose between Nina's Devil and her God, both demanding, untrustworthy, and not, by their nature, on her side. This certainly represented in global form Nina's experience of her mother:

when she pleased her mother, her mother was all smiles and praise, but her mother's narcissism needed a "perfect" daughter (which meant a mirror image of her mother's own ego ideal). So, just to be herself displeased her mother, and Nina was then ruthlessly punished. She learnt, in Winnicott's terminology, to hide her true self (Winnicott, 1960, p. 142).

This psychological split between the good parent and the bad is how Freud understood our creation of both God and Devil: the father we love and admire is projected into God, and the father we hate and fear is projected into the Devil; we cannot have one without the other (Freud, 1923d, pp. 85–86; cf. Rizzuto, 1979, p. 20).

In Hindu mythology, by contrast, the God of destruction is one aspect of the God of creation, and this is not necessarily about destroying something bad: it is the inevitable turning of the cycle of life and death. But, in Hindu stories, as in Buddhist stories, there are also evil beings that need to be destroyed. These are often depicted as monsters who entrap and attack the hero on his path to salvation, or glory, or mastery of his own life. Contemporary Eastern devotees often understand these monsters as symbols of our uncontrolled passions, which do attack and can destroy our conscious wishes. Similarly, modern Western psychologists understand that what we experience as evil non-human beings are projections of our own self-destructive powers. Without using any religious vocabulary, this was much how Nina's therapist understood her relationship to her Devil.

In Western religious tradition, the Devil evolved slowly. In the Hebrew *Bible* (roughly the same in content as the Christian Old Testament), not much place is given to a devil. It is God who, in a fit of rage, drowns all the people except Noah and his family. In *The Torah* (the rabbinical commentary on this *Bible*), "devils" are pagan Gods or a person who is an enemy or accuser. Satan the tempter comes to prominence only in the Book of Job, written sometime between the seventh and the second century BCE. The Hebrew *Bible* generally attributes to the human being the human decision, such as Jonah's when he tries to avoid going to Nineveh as God had commanded: Jonah did not wish to preach repentance to his enemies, the people of Nineveh, and thereby save them from the wrath of God; he wanted them to suffer that wrath.

Christians and Muslims, however, have a well-defined Devil and a well-defined hell. The Christian Devil and hell, in the form now generally known, originate not so much in the Christian *Bible* as in medieval tradition, but in *The Koran*, revealed and written down in the seventh century CE, Satan and hell are already prominent. Satan appears in the story of the Fall of Adam and Eve only in *The Koran*. For Hindus and Buddhists, the doctrine of reincarnation is more like the Christian doctrine of Purgatory, in that people are given another chance to do better. It is clearly important that the therapist listens carefully to what the Devil, or the power of evil, or the fear of punishment, or death as an escape from the traumas of living, means to this patient now; it varies enormously from one tradition to another, as well as in people's personal experiences.

Winnicott approaches the fact of evil from the perspective of child development. For him there is no Devil.

> [A]ll sorts of feelings and ideas of goodness that belong to the child
> . . . can be put out there and labelled 'God'. In the same way, nastiness
> in the child can be called 'the devil and all his works'. The labelling
> socializes the otherwise personal phenomenon . . . and deplete[s] the
> individual of individual creativeness. [Winnicott, 1963b, p. 95]

If the child has not been loved enough, then "compliance and false socialization" are possible, but these are manifestations of despair. For such a child, to be his true self necessitates "aggressive behaviour, destructive acts and compulsive cruelty, and perversions", which arise out of the "painful confusional clinical state" of the child, and which indicate that he still has some hope of being understood. To be his true self, then, he needs to be a little devil.

When such behaviour continues into adulthood and leads to criminal acts, even murder, the person is "wicked" in the eyes of society, but to the psychoanalyst he is "ill" (*ibid.*, pp. 103–104). Not only forensic psychiatrists in the criminal justice system find themselves working with such an adult. A therapist in private practice or in the NHS, for instance, might well find himself working with someone whom he considers is cruel to her children, perhaps a patient who thinks such behaviour is normal. And while we need to be aware in such situations of our legal responsibilities to those who could be harmed, we also need to be able to understand how we can fulfil our clinical responsibility to our patient. Winnicott can help us here.

Bion, very similarly, considers that what the baby's mother has not understood and contained is projected as the baby's mode of defence.

Although he does not write about the Devil, in his theory of the projection of Beta elements he shows how a Devil could be constructed (Bion, 1962, pp. 112–117). He imagines the young child expelling persecutory material into a host of external objects, where, fragmented, they can torment him, at the extreme in a psychotic delusional form, as Malcolm thought the town councillors were Devils persecuting him with their evil policy. The consequences of an unempathic not-me experienced too soon and too forcefully—what Winnicott calls "impingements"—haunt and persecute Bion's adult in a world of paranoia, filling him with terror and dread. In delusional psychotic mode, this can be experienced as persecution by an actual Devil.

For Jung, however, the Devil has an existence in his own right. It is our Shadow, our unconsciousness, which can act with power and autonomy. Jung defines "demonism" as consisting in the annihilation of the ego by an unconscious complex which dominates the psyche (Jung, 1945, p. 648). This is how Malcolm's therapist understood his possession. In some spiritual language today, as frequently in previous times, such loss of ego means the subject is possessed by the Devil, and exorcism can then be the therapy of choice, even if it leads to the death of the possessed. This is relevant not only to spiritual beliefs emanating from Africa and South America; a man who was in a German Catholic orphanage in the 1970s reports how the visiting priest would beat him, shouting, "I'll soon drive Satan out of you!" (Boyes, 2010).

Conclusion

The myth of the hero is very attractive, very useful, and very dangerous. It can lead us to ambitions, hopes, and challenges, for ourselves and in altruism also for others. But we can all too easily identify with the hero, and then our self is depleted outside this myth; we cannot be a hero all the time. Even more extreme, we can be possessed by the saviour complex and lose touch with reality. Jung had a dream, in 1913, in which he had to kill the hero Siegfried. He understood this dream as his need to kill off the identification in himself with his hero complex, and to acknowledge that there were many forces in his unconscious psyche over which his ego's will had no control (Jung, 1962, p. 205).

CHAPTER EIGHT

Conclusion

"The way that can be spoken of is not the constant way; the name that can be named is not the constant name"

(The Tao, 1963, Section 1)

Psychotherapy, New Age, and traditional spirituality

Religious beliefs and practices can be psychological aids towards giving our life meaning and significance; that is, a religion can act as a directional guide and a container for our spiritual needs. Psychotherapy similarly can meet and contain our spiritual needs. This does not mean that psychotherapy is a religion, though some people see it as a cult, trying to convert and retain neophytes. In health, the aim of a therapy is to free the patient from the person of the therapist and from psychotherapy itself; a religion offers a lifelong relationship.

There are many other guides and containers, as we have seen, for what Jung calls the process of individuation: a person being not-divided from parts of themselves, and so becoming the true and full individual they potentially are (Jung, 1928, par. 266). This is the goal, but "[t]he goal is important only as an idea; the essential thing is the *opus* which leads to the goal: *that* is the goal of a lifetime" (Jung, 1946, par. 400).

In psychological ill health, the goal can be perverted to innumerable variants on narcissistic satisfactions, from which none of us is ever entirely free (cf. Introduction). Whether religious or not, we are all always recovering sinners. There is always the need to integrate the more unpleasant aspects of our Shadow. Those who consider the focus on self in therapy as self-indulgent and selfish seem to assume that becoming who a person most deeply and truly is will be necessarily a delightful and welcome revelation. Some New Age spirituality focuses exclusively on love and happiness, though much of it is also lived out in the tough reality of living in the community or in campaigning for local or international peace or justice.

Some spiritual and religious templates from the past can help us tune in to the depth of the transformation some of our patients seek. At the end of Aeschylus's trilogy *The Oresteia*, the Shadow is integrated into the individual psyche of Orestes and into the collective psyche of the state. Orestes has taken responsibility for the murder of his mother and her lover, and the Furies (his guilt externalized) are transformed into the Kindly Ones, and have a special place designated for them under the city of Athens, where they are honoured (cf. Clark, 2009, pp. 242–244). Integrating the Shadow seems central also to the death and resurrection stories which abound in the Middle East in the Axial Age (ca. 800–200 BCE). The god who has been killed comes back to life and makes the earth fruitful. These stories speak of hope that, after what seems like failure, a person can rise again to a new and fruitful life. The story of the Buddha is similarly the story of a man who wanted to expand his conscious awareness and his psychic strength so that he could contemplate all of life unafraid. He needed to find a meaning in his own life for old age, sickness, and death.

This quest, imaged in the quest for the Holy Grail, is not a new, selfishly individualistic notion of the twentieth century, fashioned by people who no longer felt the need to struggle for physical survival and to maintain the cohesiveness of the group. It is an urge, a purposefulness, which we can trace back as far as history opens the way. The longing for spiritual satisfaction is, as Jung said, a force as real as hunger and the fear of death (Jung, 1928, par. 403). When one form of satisfying our spiritual needs does not work, we seek another. We might change the language, but the intention is the same; it is about finding meaning and purpose in our lives.

Clinical example: Olivia—spirituality and relationships

Olivia was a witch. She came into therapy when her toddler daughter was killed, while out with her husband, when a motorbike went out of control and mounted the pavement. Her husband also had a motorbike, and Olivia unconsciously identified him with the rider who had killed their daughter, and she could not forgive him. She had long been afraid that he would himself die in a motorbike accident.

She was a primary school teacher, good at her job; she got on well with colleagues and with parents, as well as with the children. Her curly dark hair was pulled back from her face, and she wore clothes which fascinated her therapist: full skirts with symbols embroidered on them, or with bands of colour, and multi-coloured tops, often with a large necklace with a pendant which he thought was probably symbolic for her.

At first, it did not seem that her being a witch was relevant to the course of the therapy. She needed to grieve, and be angry. She needed to find out if she could stay with her husband when she blamed him so unforgivingly; she needed to find out why she had been angry with him for so long anyway, expressed in her fear that he would himself die in a motorbike accident; she needed to find out how to love her little son, whom she said had always been closer to his father. She ran the risk of losing all her family, not just her daughter.

Her therapist, who knew nothing about witches except what Olivia told him, and deliberately did not do any research to find out, wondered if her beliefs would be of any spiritual help to her, help about forgiveness, or about what happened after death, or about what the purpose of her daughter's short life might be. When she spoke of her desolate weekends, he approached this area by asking if she had a meeting of her coven to go to. But he reached another area entirely: he learnt that her husband disapproved of her being a witch, that he associated it with being lesbian and crazy, and that he feared for their marriage because of her involvement. Olivia, rather similarly, saw her husband's motorbike as a rejection of her and a retreat to a macho, matey male culture which excluded women. Olivia had become a witch six years previously, when her father died; her mother was a lapsed Catholic. Her therapist found that, as so often, the significance of Olivia's spiritual practices was inextricably bound up with her family relationships. It was work on these relationships, and on what being a witch meant to her, rather than on witchcraft itself, which was the focus of the therapy.

Fundamentalist believers

We can understand why fundamentalist believers in the tradition of the monotheistic Judaic religions—Judaism, Christianity, and Islam—are usually hostile to psychotherapy. Far from seeing depth psychology as a helpful way of understanding and explaining the religious and spiritual truths they believe in, as many more liberal theologians do, they see it as an enemy, undermining what they need to experience as facts. Such people give the impression of being imprisoned in the paranoid–schizoid position, where there is no symbolic function. A patient in such a psychic state needs careful containment; indeed, pyschodynamic psychotherapy is likely to be contra-indicated, since the belief structure is often holding the personality together. However, sometimes a patient may present with a fundamentalist psychic "pocket", such as a belief in creationist theory, when the therapist's understanding and respect for the particular psychic needs this is serving might enable useful work to be done in other areas.

Sometimes, it is the therapist who is fundamentalist. This is a problem only if she regards it as part of her therapeutic task to convert her patient to her point of view. This applies to both religious fundamentalism and to a fundamentalist belief in a particular "church" of psychotherapy. A fundamentalist Christian therapist might see it as her vocation to try to change her patient's sexual orientation, if it does not agree with her reading of The Bible. Equally, a convinced atheist might see it as her mission to wean her patient from what she considers an infantile dependence on an illusion—a belief in God. And non-psychodynamic work might muddle the transference with the therapist praying with the patient in a session, or attempting to heal him with the laying on of hands.

The therapist's own belief system

It will have become clear throughout this monograph that the essential way of understanding spirituality and religion in clinical practice is to understand them in exactly the same way as understanding any other material. That is all. What the therapist herself believes or practises or despises or regrets or is tempted by or is awed by or dallies with in these spheres is relevant only in so far as she cannot separate them from her patient's concerns.

But there is always the potential for our inadequately considered legacy from Freud to influence our clinical work. The main danger is that our minds will be closed to an examination of what "God" means to this particular patient, and of the purpose that this belief currently serves. A patient starts going to church again as he did as a child. Maybe he is regressing to childhood behaviour, maybe he is returning to the customs of his parents, or maybe he is striking out in a way which would have appalled them. Any of these things also might in themselves be positive or, on the contrary, be less helpful steps. Context and meaning are everything. The act itself tells us very little.

It is not our business as therapists to think of "true" or "false" when we encounter our patient's images of God. How would we know, anyway? Our business is to understand how that image developed, where it came from, and in what ways it facilitates or hinders the patient's moving towards greater self-realization, a greater experience of reality in his relations to his own internal state and to the external world. This judgement is not a simple matter, but it is a frequent dilemma in many areas of our work. We can never be a neutral, non-influencing presence.

Conclusion

Psychotherapy, like a religion, is trying to make sense of the practical and spiritual aspects of ordinary life, to link the known and the unknown, to cope with hopes and fears about ultimate questions: what does my being alive mean? What purpose does my life have? Does anyone care? Is there life after death? Why does love matter? Why is there so much suffering? Why am I and other people so needlessly cruel? Existential, spiritual questions.

REFERENCES

Abram, J. (1996). *The Language of Winnicott*. London: Karnac.

Armstrong, K. (1981). *Through the Narrow Gate*. London: Macmillan [revised edition London: Flamingo, 1997].

Armstrong, K. (1993). *A History of God*. London: Heinemann [reprinted London: Mandarin Paperbacks, 1994].

Bettelheim, B. (1982). *Freud and Man's Soul*. New York: Knopf.

Bion, W. R. (1958). On hallucination. In: *Second Thoughts* (pp. 65–85). London: Heinemann, 1967.

Bion, W. R. (1962). A theory of thinking. In: *Second Thoughts* (pp. 110–119). London: Heinemann, 1967.

Bion, W. R. (1970). *Attention and Interpretation*. London: Tavistock.

Black, D. M. (1993). What sort of thing is a religion? A view from object-relations theory. *International Journal of Psycho-Analysis, 74*: 613–625.

Black, D. M. (Ed.) (2006). *Psychoanalysis and Religion in the 21st Century: Competitors or Collaborators?* London: Routledge.

Bollas, C. (1987). *The Shadow of the Object: Psychoanalysis of the Unthought Known*. London: Free Association Books.

Bomford, R. (1999). *The Symmetry of God*. London: Free Association Books.

Boyes, R. (2010). Pope's ally accused of beating children with sticks and fists. *The Times*, 1 April.

Brown, D. (2003). *The Da Vinci Code*. London: Bantam Press.

Brown, R., & Stobart, K. (2008). *Understanding Boundaries in Clinical Practice*. London: Karnac.

Capra, F. (1975). *The Tao of Physics*. London: Wildwood House [reprinted London: Flamingo, 1983].

Clark, M. (2009). Suppose Freud had chosen Orestes instead. *Journal of Analytical Psychology*, 54: 233–252.

Edinger, E. F. (1987). *The Christian Archetype*. Toronto: Inner City Books.

Edmundson, M. (1990). *Towards Reading Freud*. Princeton, CT: Princeton University Press [reprinted Chicago, IL: University of Chicago Press, 2007].

Eigen, M. (1998). *The Psychoanalytic Mystic*. London: Free Association Books.

Fowler, J. W. (1981). *Stages of Faith*. San Francisco, CA: HarperCollins.

Freud, S. (1907b). Obsessive actions and religious practices. *S.E.*, 9: 115–127. London: Hogarth.

Freud, S. (1912–1913). *Totem and Taboo*. *S.E.*, 13: 1–161. London: Hogarth.

Freud, S. (1923d). A seventeenth century demonological neurosis. *S.E.*, 19: 69–105. London: Hogarth.

Freud, S. (1925d). An autobiographical study. *S.E.*, 20: 1–74. London: Hogarth.

Freud, S. (1927c). *The Future of an Illusion*. *S.E.*, 21: 1–56. London: Hogarth.

Freud, S. (1930a). Civilization and its Discontents. *S.E.*, 21: 57–145. London: Hogarth.

Freud, S. (1939a). *Moses and Monotheism*. *S.E.*, 23: 3–138. London: Hogarth.

Freud, S. (1961). *Letters of Sigmund Freud 1873–1939*, E. L. Freud (Ed.). London: Hogarth.

Fromm, E. (1960). *Psycho-Analysis and Zen Buddhism*. Sydney: George Allen & Unwin.

Gay, P. (1988). *Freud: A Life For Our Time*. New York: W. W. Norton [reprinted in paperback, 1998].

Gruber, A. (2009). A transpersonal integrative approach to child psychotherapy. *The Psychotherapist*, 41: 31–33.

Hampson, D. (1990). *Theology and Feminism*. Oxford: Blackwell.

Harlow, P. (1996). Malign individuation. Paper read to the Society of Analytical Psychology (unpublished).

Homer (1950). *The Iliad*, E. V. Rieu (Trans.). London: Penguin.

Hopkins, G. M. (1877). Hurrahing in harvest. In: W. H. Gardner (Ed.), *Poems and Prose of Gerard Manley Hopkins* (p. 31). Harmondsworth: Penguin, 1953.

Jacobs, M. (1993). *Living Illusions*. London: Society for Promoting Christian Knowledge.

James, W. (1902). *The Varieties of Religious Experience* [reprinted London: Penguin Classics, 1985].

Jones, E. (1953). *Sigmund Freud Life and Work, Vol. 1: The Young Freud 1856–1900*. London: Hogarth.

Jones, E. (1955). *Sigmund Freud Life and Work, Vol. 2: Years of Maturity 1901–1919*. London: Hogarth.

Julian of Norwich (1978). *Showings*, E. Colledge & J. Walsh (Eds.). New York: Paulist Press.

Jung, C. G. (1921). *Psychological Types*. C.W., 6. London: Routledge & Kegan Paul.

Jung, C. G. (1928). The relations between the ego and the unconscious, C.W., 7: 123–241. London: Routledge & Kegan Paul.

Jung, C. G. (1931). Commentary on *The Secret of the Golden Flower*, C.W., 13: 1–55. London: Routledge & Kegan Paul.

Jung, C. G. (1932). Psychotherapists or the clergy, C.W., 11: 327–347. London: Routledge & Kegan Paul.

Jung, C. G. (1935). Principles of practical psychotherapy, C.W., 16: 3–20. London: Routledge & Kegan Paul.

Jung, C. G. (1938[1954]). Psychological aspects of the mother archetype, C.W., 9.i: 75–110. London: Routledge & Kegan Paul.

Jung, C. G. (1940). Psychology and religion, C.W., 11: 3–105. London: Routledge & Kegan Paul.

Jung, C. G. (1940[1941]).Transformation symbolism in the Mass, C.W., 11: 201–296. London: Routledge & Kegan Paul.

Jung, C. G. (1941). The psychology of the child archetype, C.W., 9.i: 151–181. London: Routledge & Kegan Paul.

Jung, C. G. (1942). A psychological approach to the dogma of the Trinity, C.W., 11: 107–200. London: Routledge & Kegan Paul.

Jung, C. G. (1944). *Psychology and Alchemy*. C.W., 12. London: Routledge & Kegan Paul.

Jung, C. G. (1945). The definition of demonism, C.W., 18: 648. London: Routledge & Kegan Paul.

Jung, C. G. (1946). The psychology of the transference, C.W., 16: 163–323. London: Routledge & Kegan Paul.

Jung, C. G. (1951). *Aion*. C.W., 9.ii. London: Routledge & Kegan Paul.

Jung, C. G. (1952). Answer to Job, C.W., 11: 355–470. London: Routledge & Kegan Paul.

Jung, C. G. (1962). *Memories, Dreams, Reflections*. New York: Pantheon [reprinted London: Fontana Paperbacks, 1983].

Jung, C. G. (2009). *The Red Book*, S. Shamdasani (Ed.). New York: W. W. Norton.

Kalsched, D. (1996). *The Inner World of Trauma*. London: Routledge.

Knox, J. (2009). Mirror neurons and embodied simulation in the development of archetypes and self-agency. *Journal of Analytical Psychology, 54*: 307–323.

Kristeva, J. (1987). *In the Beginning Was Love: Psychoanalysis and Faith*, A. Goldhammer (Trans.). New York: Columbia University Press.

MacKenna, C. (2002). Self images and God images. *British Journal of Psychotherapy, 18*(3): 325–338.

Mahabharata (1999). K. Dharma (Trans.). Canada: Torchlight Publishing.

Mantel, H. (2005). *Beyond Black*. London: Harper Perennial.

Mathers, D., Miller, M. E., & Ando, O. (Eds.) (2009). *Self and No-Self*. London: Routledge.

Meissner, W. W. (1984). *Psychoanalysis and Religious Experience*. New Haven: Yale University Press.

Meltzer, D. (1988). *The Apprehension of Beauty*. Strath Tay, Perthshire: Clunie Press.

Molino, A. (Ed.) (1998). *The Couch and the Tree*. USA: North Point Press.

Mookerjee, A. (1988). *Kali: The Feminine Force*. London: Thames and Hudson.

Neumann, E. (1954). *The Origins and History of Consciousness*. Princeton, CT: Princeton University Press.

Orwell, G. (1949). *Nineteen Eighty-Four*. London: Secker and Warburg [reprinted London: Penguin, 1954].

Palmer, M. (1997). *Freud and Jung on Religion*. London: Routledge.

Redfearn, J. W. T. (1985). *My Self, My Many Selves*. London: Academic Press.

Rizzuto, A.-M. (1979). *The Birth of the Living God*. Chicago, IL: University of Chicago Press.

Robinson, H., & Fuller, V. G. (2003). *Understanding Narcissism in Clinical Practice*. London: Karnac.

Rumi (2004). *Selected Poems*, C. Banks (Trans.). London: Penguin.

Rycroft, C. (1968). *A Critical Dictionary of Psychoanalysis*. London: Nelson.

Samuels, A., Shorter, B., & Plaut, F. (1986). *A Critical Dictionary of Jungian Analysis*. London: Routledge & Kegan Paul.

Schreurs, A. (2002). *Psychotherapy and Spirituality*. London: Jessica Kingsley.

Shakespeare, W. (1967). *A Midsummer Night's Dream*, S. Wells (Ed.). London: Penguin.

Shamdasani, S. (2003). *Jung and the Making of Modern Psychology: The Dream of a Science*. Cambridge: Cambridge University Press.

Snelling, J. (1987). *The Buddhist Handbook*. London: Rider [reprinted London: Rider, 1998].

Symington, N. (1994). *Emotion and Spirit: Questioning the Claims of Psychoanalysis and Religion*. London: Cassell.

Tao Te Ching (1963). D. C. Lau (Trans.). London: Penguin.

The Bible (1989). New Revised Standard Version, anglicized edition. Oxford: Oxford University Press.

The Koran (1998). N. J. Dawood (Trans.). London: Penguin.

Traherne, T. (1934). *Felicities*, A. Quiller-Couch (Ed.). London: P. J. & A. E. Dobell.

von Franz, M.-L. (1970). *An Introduction to the Interpretation of Fairytales*. New York: Spring.

von Franz, M.-L. (1974). *Shadow and Evil in Fairytales*. New York: Spring.

Williams, R. (2003). *Silence and Honey Cakes*. Oxford: Lion Hudson.

Winnicott, D. W. (1953). Transitional objects and transitional phenomena. In: *Playing and Reality* (pp. 1–30). London: Tavistock, 1971 [reprinted London: Pelican, 1974].

Winnicott, D. W. (1960). Ego distortion in terms of true and false self. In: *The Maturational Processes and the Facilitating Environment* (pp. 140–152). London: Hogarth, 1965.

Winnicott, D. W. (1963a). Communicating and not communicating leading to a study of certain opposites. In: *The Maturational Processes and the Facilitating Environment* (pp. 179–192). London: Hogarth, 1965.

Winnicott, D. W. (1963b). Morals and education. In: *The Maturational Processes and the Facilitating Environment* (pp. 93–105). London: Hogarth, 1965.

Winnicott, D. W. (1967). The location of cultural experience. In: *Playing and Reality* (pp. 112–121). London: Tavistock, 1971 [reprinted London: Pelican, 1974].

Winnicott, D. W. (1968). Playing and culture. In: C. Winnicott (Ed.), *Psycho-Analytic Explorations* (pp. 203–207). London: Karnac, 1989.

Winnicott, D. W. (1971). The place where we live. In: *Playing and Reality* (pp. 122–129). London: Tavistock, 1971 [reprinted London: Pelican, 1974].

Wordsworth, W. (1975). Elegiac stanzas suggested by a picture of Peele castle. In: W. Davies (Ed.), *William Wordsworth: Selected Poems* (pp. 126–127). London: J. M. Dent & Sons.

Zohar, D. (1990). *The Quantum Self*. London: Bloomsbury [reprinted London: Flamingo, 1991].

INDEX

id, 5
Institute of Psychoanalysis, 10
International Association for
   Psycho-Analysis, 4
Islam, xiii, xvi, 1, 8, 22, 24, 38–39,
   53–54, 79, 86 *see also*:
   Devil/Satan, hell, *The Koran*

Jacobs, M., 29, 91
James, W., 44, 91
Jones, E., 3–4, 91
Judaism, xiii, xvi–xvii, 1, 3–5, 10, 19,
   24, 35, 38, 86
Julian of Norwich, 62, 91
Jung, C. G., x–xi, xviii, 2, 4, 11–12,
   14–16, 18–20, 31, 46, 54, 65, 81,
   83–84, 91–92

Kalsched, D., 59, 92
Knox, J., 46, 92
Kristeva, J., 10, 92

life *see also*: death
   adult, 23, 34, 37, 45–46
   external, 47, 52
   ordinary, 17, 35, 49, 52, 87
   social, 6, 58

MacKenna, C., 31, 92
Maeder, A., 2
Magic Flute, The see: Mozart, W. A.
Mahabharata, 62, 64, 92
Mantel, H., 62, 92
Mathers, D., 20, 92
Matte Blanco, I., 45
meditation, 13–14, 36, 49, 53–54
Meissner, W. W., 10, 27–28, 45, 92
Meltzer, D., 47, 92
Michelangelo, 69
Miller, M. E., 20, 92
Molino, A., 20, 92
Mookerjee, A., 22, 92
mourn *see*: bereavement
Mozart, W. A., 49
mystical experience(s), xiv, xviii, 28,
   43–47, 54–55

mythology/myths, 14, 16, 20, 46, 69,
   75–76, 79, 81 *see also*: Oedipus
   complex
Orestes, 84
Osiris, 18

narcissism, 5–6, 17, 39, 48, 74–75, 79,
   84
National Health Service (NHS), 6, 25,
   59, 63, 80
   Day Centre, 64
Nazis, 4, 31, 37, 70
Neumann, E., 19, 92
neurosis, xiii, 57, 60, 64
   compulsive, 8
   obsessional, 1, 3, 8
New Age, xviii, 83–84

object
   external, 81
   good, 34
   internal, xii, 23, 28–29, 34, 54, 74
   primary, 27
   relations, xii, 29
   self, 71
   transitional, 34–37
objective/objectivity, xvi, 2, 34, 62,
   70
obsessive(ness), 6, 8–9, 55, 75
Oedipal ideas, xii, 1, 25–26
Oedipus complex, 1–3, 10
Orwell, G., 38–39, 92
Oxfam, 75

Palmer, M., 20, 92
personality disorder, 61, 63
phantasy, 3, 75–76
Plato, 47
Plaut, F., x, 16, 92
projection, 2–3, 6, 14–16, 22, 35, 46,
   51, 59, 62, 66, 71, 74–75, 79–81
projective identification, 46, 65

Redfearn, J. W. T., 61, 92
religion, xi–xiii, xv–xviii, 1–3, 5, 8,
   10–16, 19–21, 23–24, 29–31,